Prezi Essentials

Create dynamic, engaging, and beautiful presentations
on your journey through Prezi

Domi Sinclair

BIRMINGHAM - MUMBAI

Prezi Essentials

First published: September 2014

Production reference: 1160914

Published by Packt Publishing Ltd.
Livery Place
35 Livery Street
Birmingham B3 2PB, UK.

ISBN 978-1-78355-293-1

www.packtpub.com

Cover image by Ravaji Babu (ravaji_babu@outlook.com)

Credits

Author
Domi Sinclair

Reviewers
Marthe Bijman
David Hopkins
J.J. Sylvia IV

Commissioning Editor
Kunal Parikh

Acquisition Editor
Neha Nagwekar

Content Development Editor
Poonam Jain

Technical Editor
Taabish Khan

Copy Editors
Dipti Kapadia
Laxmi Subramanian

Project Coordinator
Mary Alex

Proofreaders
Simran Bhogal
Maria Gould
Ameesha Green

Indexer
Tejal Soni

Production Coordinator
Saiprasad Kadam

Cover Work
Saiprasad Kadam

About the Author

Domi Sinclair is a Learning Technologist at University College, London. This role requires her to advise educators on the use of a range of technology-enhanced learning solutions including social media and collaboration platforms such as Prezi. She has an undergraduate degree in Journalism and a Master's degree in Media, both of which required her to use innovative platforms and hone her presentation skills. It was through this desire to stand out during presentations that she first discovered the Prezi platform, and she has been utilizing it ever since. She has presented at a number of national and international conferences on both sides of the Atlantic. She always favors using the Prezi platform to compliment face-to-face presentations and has converted a number of her team's shared presentations from PowerPoint to Prezi.

Domi has authored the book, *Instant Prezi for Education How-to, Packt Publishing,* which was released last year.

Acknowledgments

First, thanks to the brilliant team at Packt Publishing who have been very helpful and have worked hard to get this title out. I would also like to thank the technical reviewers for their candid feedback, which has not only helped improve this title but also my skills as an author.

This book is dedicated to 'Nanny', my proud grandmother, who has been cheerleading my previous title to anyone who will listen, despite never having used a computer herself! It is her support, as well as that of my husband, parents, brother, in-laws, and friends that has helped me get to the stage where I am. Their love and encouragement inspires me every day. I am lucky to have such wonderful people in my life, without whom I may not have been in a position to access technology or write books.

About the Reviewers

Marthe Bijman is a writer, literature critic, and marketing communications specialist. She has worked extensively in the mining and information technology industries. She holds a BA degree, BA (Honors) in Literature, BA (Honors) in Journalism, HDipEd in Language Teaching, and an MA in Applied Linguistics and Literary Sciences. She publishes book reviews and analyses on her literary blog, `http://www.sevencircumstances.com`. Her blog on business writing and marketing is at `http://www.red-pennant-communications.com`. In collaboration with her husband, she is the author and designer of self-published photography as well as reference and poetry books, featured on `http://www.blurb.com`. South Africa-born, she now lives and works in Vancouver, Canada.

David Hopkins is an experienced and respected eLearning consultant at Warwick Business School. His work and research centers around the use of appropriate technology for, and with, students, both online and on-campus. From a background in commercial Internet technologies and online communities, he applies his knowledge and experience to eLearning pedagogy to bring effective and appropriate use of technology in effective learning experiences. His current interests and research are based around the use of mobile devices for online learning (for both campus and distance learners) and the use of social media and social networks for effective communication and collaboration between staff, students, and his peers. He is a regular blogger (`http://www.dontwasteyourtime.co.uk`) on the aspects of learning technology, CMS/VLEs, social networks, and other aspects of the utilization of technology in a pedagogic environment. He started blogging about his experiences and activities in 2008, but has been an advocate of blogging and online communities from as far back as 1999, and his first role was of a web designer.

Prezi has long been David's passion, and he offers Prezi workshops to academic staff and students alike, enabling students to leave higher education ready for the modern office environment, giving them skills and knowledge to incorporate new technologies and new approaches to existing technology in the workplace.

J.J. Sylvia IV is a PhD student in the Communication, Rhetoric, and Digital Media program at North Carolina State University. He also has an MA in Philosophy from the University of Southern Mississippi and BA degrees in Philosophy and Communication from Mississippi State University. His experience spans the fields of business, education, and non-profits, which has given him the opportunity to develop a unique perspective on the way people use and engage with technology.

His primary research interests revolve around how datafication affects our understanding and our interactions with the world around us. He strives to create new ways of presenting and visualizing this data so that it is helpful and productive for Humanities and Social Sciences. Before graduate school, he managed paid advertising and marketing strategies for an e-commerce site and developed a social media outreach initiative for a non-profit organization. Most recently, he managed AmeriCorps interns who worked to integrate technology in the classroom and built a community around an educational outreach blog, `http://www.PhilosophyMatters.org`. He can also be found at `http://www.jjsylvia.com`.

J.J. has reviewed the book, *Prezi Hotshot, Hedwyg van Groenendaal, Packt Publishing*. He has published chapters in books such as *Ethical Issues in E-Business, Daniel E. Palmer, Business Science Reference*; *Radiohead and Philosophy, Brandon W. Forbes and George A. Reisch*; *Doctor Who and Philosophy, Courtland Lewis and Paula Smithka*; and *Supervillains and Philosophy, Ben Dyer*, all published by Open Court.

www.PacktPub.com

Support files, eBooks, discount offers, and more

You might want to visit www.PacktPub.com for support files and downloads related to your book.

Did you know that Packt offers eBook versions of every book published, with PDF and ePub files available? You can upgrade to the eBook version at www.PacktPub.com and as a print book customer, you are entitled to a discount on the eBook copy. Get in touch with us at service@packtpub.com for more details.

At www.PacktPub.com, you can also read a collection of free technical articles, sign up for a range of free newsletters and receive exclusive discounts and offers on Packt books and eBooks.

http://PacktLib.PacktPub.com

Do you need instant solutions to your IT questions? PacktLib is Packt's online digital book library. Here, you can access, read and search across Packt's entire library of books.

Why subscribe?

- Fully searchable across every book published by Packt
- Copy and paste, print and bookmark content
- On demand and accessible via web browser

Free access for Packt account holders

If you have an account with Packt at www.PacktPub.com, you can use this to access PacktLib today and view nine entirely free books. Simply use your login credentials for immediate access.

Table of Contents

Preface

Prezi is an online presentation and collaboration tool. Unlike traditional tools, it allows you to have complete control of how the content is arranged, meaning you can break free from the traditional linear pattern. This enables a presentation of information that reflects patterns of thoughts, utilizes design skills, and highlights patterns of information. This new way of laying out information also makes movement through the presentation more dynamic and engaging for the audience.

Alongside an exciting new way of presenting, Prezi makes it easy to upload and embed your own custom content and external media. This book will guide you through all of this as well as working with external graphics programs such as Adobe Illustrator. This book will also explore the customization of themes and CSS code for Prezi presentations. So, with *Prezi Essentials* giving you the technical skills, the only limits will be your own creativity.

What this book covers

Chapter 1, Introduction, gets you started with Prezi including which account type to choose.

Chapter 2, Working with What You've Got, teaches you how to create a new presentation from a template and import your PowerPoint slides.

Chapter 3, Creating Something New, explains how to start a Prezi from scratch, add basic content, and customize themes or CSS code.

Chapter 4, Using Existing Content, brings your own custom content into Prezi including complex graphics and external media.

Chapter 5, Working with External Packages, enables an exploration of how to prepare content from packages, such as Adobe Illustrator, for Prezi including which file formats to use.

Chapter 6, Making it Work Together, explains how to tie your presentation together by learning how to group content, and add paths and timings to your presentation.

Chapter 7, Collaborating, helps you take Prezi to the next level by discovering how you can use it to work with others on your project right from creation to finally presenting it.

What you need for this book

- A computer or laptop (with mouse, keyboard, speakers, and ideally a microphone)

- A comfortable space to work

- Some materials to work with (images, videos, and audio files)

- An Internet connection

- Flash version 11.1

- An up-to-date web browser (Internet Explorer, Mozilla Firefox, Google Chrome, and Safari are all compatible)

Who this book is for

This book is intended for individuals who want to learn Prezi, and specifically how to design within Prezi. Perhaps you already know a bit about Prezi, but have never used it; or perhaps you have used Prezi before but want to learn how to incorporate your own custom design elements. In either case, this book will get you up and running quickly. It would be helpful to have a bit of familiarity with basic design concepts and the use of Prezi, but prior experience is not essential.

Conventions

In this book, you will find a number of styles of text that distinguish between different kinds of information. Here are some examples of these styles, and an explanation of their meaning.

Code words in text, database table names, folder names, filenames, file extensions, pathnames, dummy URLs, user input, and Twitter handles are shown as follows: "Now, we need to export the image to a `.swf` file."

A block of code is set as follows:

```
frame.circle
{
  borderColor: #fff;
  borderThickness: 0;
  gradEndColor: #ffc7e6;
  gradStartColor: #ffc7e6;
```

When we wish to draw your attention to a particular part of a code block, the relevant lines or items are set in bold:

```
frame.circle
{
  borderColor: #f66;
  borderThickness: 6;
  gradEndColor: #ffc7e6;
  gradStartColor: #ffc7e6;
```

New terms and **important words** are shown in bold. Words that you see on the screen, in menus or dialog boxes for example, appear in the text like this: "To upload a background layer, click on **Upload** and then browse for your file."

 Warnings or important notes appear in a box like this.

Reader feedback

Feedback from our readers is always welcome. Let us know what you think about this book—what you liked or may have disliked. Reader feedback is important for us to develop titles that you really get the most out of.

To send us general feedback, simply send an e-mail to feedback@packtpub.com, and mention the book title through the subject of your message.

If there is a topic that you have expertise in and you are interested in either writing or contributing to a book, see our author guide on www.packtpub.com/authors.

Customer support

Now that you are the proud owner of a Packt book, we have a number of things to help you to get the most from your purchase.

Downloading the color images of this book

We also provide you a PDF file that has color images of the screenshots/diagrams used in this book. The color images will help you better understand the changes in the output. You can download this file from: `https://www.packtpub.com/sites/default/files/downloads/2931OT_ColoredImages.pdf`.

Errata

Although we have taken every care to ensure the accuracy of our content, mistakes do happen. If you find a mistake in one of our books—maybe a mistake in the text or the code—we would be grateful if you would report this to us. By doing so, you can save other readers from frustration and help us improve subsequent versions of this book. If you find any errata, please report them by visiting `http://www.packtpub.com/support`, selecting your book, clicking on the **errata submission form** link, and entering the details of your errata. Once your errata are verified, your submission will be accepted and the errata will be uploaded to our website, or added to any list of existing errata, under the Errata section of that title.

Piracy

Piracy of copyright material on the Internet is an ongoing problem across all media. At Packt, we take the protection of our copyright and licenses very seriously. If you come across any illegal copies of our works, in any form, on the Internet, please provide us with the location address or website name immediately so that we can pursue a remedy.

Please contact us at `copyright@packtpub.com` with a link to the suspected pirated material.

We appreciate your help in protecting our authors, and our ability to bring you valuable content.

Questions

You can contact us at `questions@packtpub.com` if you are having a problem with any aspect of the book, and we will do our best to address it.

1
Introduction

Welcome to *Prezi Essentials*, your guide to designing presentations with a powerful and dynamic online tool. In this introductory chapter, we will be setting the scene and covering the following topics:

- Why use Prezi?: An exploration of some of the advantages of this tool and how it differs from traditional tools, such as PowerPoint
- Getting to know the lingo: In this section, we will explore some common terminology for Prezi
- Getting inspired: Enough talk, this section will show you what you can do, and hopefully get your creative juices flowing
- Getting started: Now that you are raring to go, this section will give you some practical tips on what you need to continue your Prezi journey
- Which account to choose?: Finally, we will look at which account types might be right for you, so you have everything you need to begin creating a Prezi presentation

Why use Prezi?

Whether you are relatively new to Prezi, or have already made a few presentations, this book aims to show you how to build a good workflow and pull content from a range of sources. It is essential that you understand how to correctly use features such as frame animations and paths, to create a seamless flow through your presentation. Inappropriate use of features such as the path to transition between frames can lead to the audience experiencing motion sickness, which is the last thing you want at a conference or business meeting.

When used correctly, the frames and paths in Prezi are part of what makes it superior to traditional presentation software such as PowerPoint. Rather than forcing the designer to use a linear format, a Prezi presentation can follow any format you wish. You can use it to express nonlinear concepts, move back and forth between frames, and build up ideas before revealing the big picture as a compilation of all the ideas explored in the presentation. This nonlinear way of presenting information also makes it easier to exit any set paths and go back to a desired frame when answering questions after delivering a presentation. Of course, even though Prezi does facilitate nonlinear presentations, you can still opt to use it in a traditional linear fashion, and you can even import your old PowerPoint slides into Prezi as a starting point. The following is a screenshot comparing the same presentation created in PowerPoint and then imported and edited in Prezi. Which one do you think looks better?

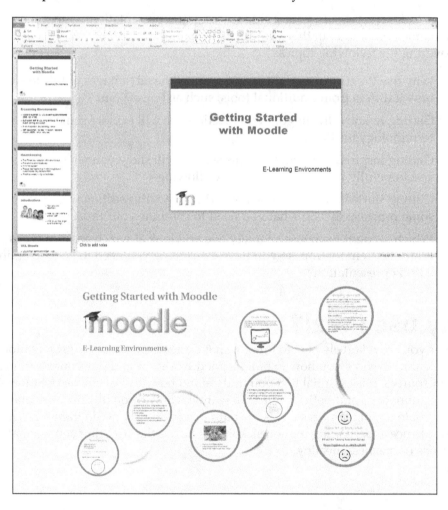

Regardless of whether you are starting from scratch or using the existing content, Prezi allows you to add or create the exact look you want via themes. These themes can be customized using the wizard interface or by editing the CSS code. Once you have designed your custom theme, you can save it for future reuse. As such, it is easy to create a corporate identity to use across a number of presentations, and it has the ability to include a company logo, which furthers the professional look of a branded presentation. Have a look at the following screenshot:

Another way Prezi can allow you to take a presentation to the next level is through the ease with which it allows you to embed multimedia content. Use images to illustrate key concepts or just to enhance the aesthetic feel of your presentation. These can be easily included using the built-in Google image search, which will allow you to filter only images licensed for commercial use. If you have created your own images, perhaps using a tool such as Adobe Illustrator, then these can be simply uploaded to Prezi—you can even choose to make them reusable in your other Prezi presentations by adding them to **My Collections**.

Alongside images, it is also easy to embed audio and video, perhaps to demonstrate an idea or to support an argument. Whether you wish to use a video already hosted online via YouTube or upload one directly into Prezi, both can be done with a few simple clicks. The following screenshot shows how you can embed both Google images and YouTube videos; it also shows how you do not need to include lots of text, as long as you have a voice-over or you are there to present the content:

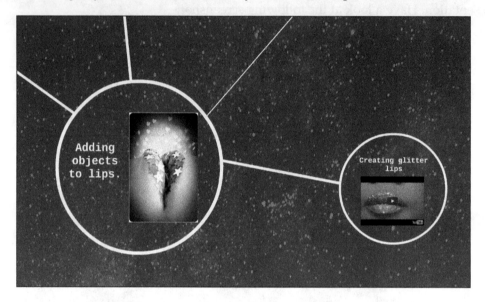

If you are working across geographic locations, you may wish to utilize the **Present remotely** feature and share your Prezi during an online meeting or via email. If you are working across time zones and are unable to present at 2 a.m., then why not utilize features such as frame-by-frame audio to narrate your presentations; that way it can be viewed without needing a live presenter.

These are some of the ways that Prezi can help enhance your work and reflect the best of your ability. It can also assist when working as part of a team by facilitating the collaborative creation of presentations with a number of editors working simultaneously to edit and add content. The friendly interface will let you see which team members are doing what within the presentation in real time.

Getting to know the lingo

To help you through this book, it might be useful to get to grips with some of the terminology used already in this book (and which will be continually used as we move through further chapters). Some of the key terms used so far are: path, canvas, and frames. In this section, we will explore what they mean. If you have used Prezi before, you may already be familiar with them. Please note: this is not a catch all guide to the terminology used in Prezi, but should explain some key terms that may be unfamiliar.

A **frame** or **frames** is the terminology used to refer to the method in Prezi for grouping content together. The easiest way to understand this is to think of frames in Prezi the same way you think of slides in PowerPoint. So, rather than a deck of slides, as you would have in PowerPoint, in Prezi, you have a series of frames.

Canvas is the word used in Prezi to describe the blank space on which you create your presentation. Much like a physical artist's canvas, you may choose to use all or part of the canvas while creating your masterpiece. Unlike a physical canvas, you can zoom into different parts and hide the parts you are not using.

Path, in the case of Prezi, refers to the preset transitions between sections or frames within the presentation. In PowerPoint, this would simply involve moving in a linear fashion from slide to slide. But as Prezi allows you to move freely around the canvas, it is necessary to determine which path you wish to take (should you wish to set one at all). Later in this book, we will discuss some of the considerations required when setting a path, such as speed of transition, and whether you wish to rotate the canvas as you transition along the path.

Getting inspired

Although this book has listed many reasons why you should use Prezi, it is often useful to see some examples of what can be done. These might inspire you with what is possible or reassure you that you can do much better. You can see many publicly available Prezi presentations on the Prezi website; they are listed under the **Explore** section and change daily. This is shown in the following screenshot:

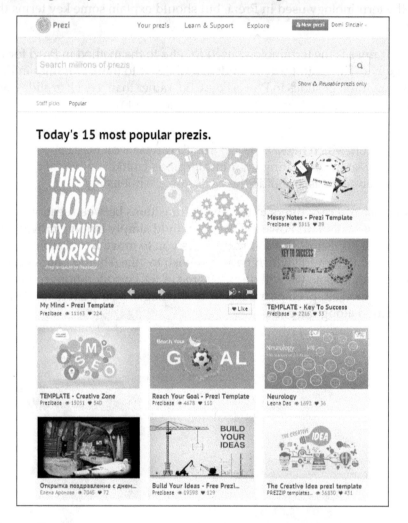

Some of the presentations listed in this area are reusable and hence might form a good starting point for your own content. Of course, you might prefer not to copy an existing presentation and just use them as stimulus for generating your own design ideas.

You can start out really basic in Prezi, simply using shapes to create an innovative or alternative nonlinear layout to your presentation, such as the following diagram that uses circular frames and lines to create a flower as the overall design. With this sort of layout, you may wish to start with an overall view, or begin zoomed into a frame and then reveal the overall concept or design only at the end. The following diagram is quite crude, but illustrates how a flower has been constructed using circular frames and some additional lines and shapes. This is a more interesting way of presenting the content than PowerPoint and will immediately gain the audience's attention and interest. You may also wish to use the created shape to make a statement about the presentation topic, for example, the many e-learning tools available in the following diagram are like petals on a flower, and it is up to you which one you pick. The color might also be important as the flower in this example is blue like a forget-me-not, which might be used to make reference to the fact that after this presentation, you will not forget about the great content.

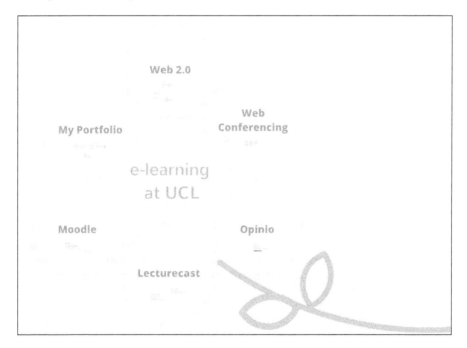

If you aren't quite ready for a nonlinear approach or perhaps your topic works best in a more linear format, then this can still be achieved in Prezi using frames. You could also consider having some text that is not part of the path, but could be accessed if required. In the following screenshot, the words under the steps are not part of the presentation path, but attention could be drawn to them when you zoom out, or the path could be left to focus on them if required by certain audiences.

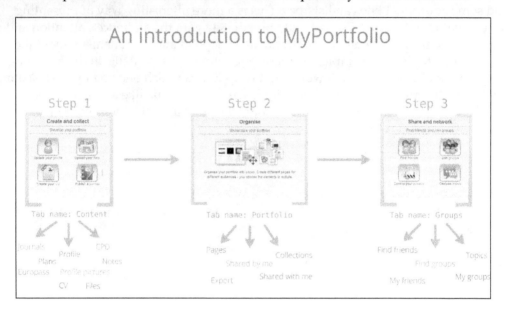

Remember as well that you may wish to utilize all of Prezi's canvas to hide and reveal content when zooming out. This might be revealed alongside the initial overview, or you could zoom into it separately. In the following screenshot, it was zoomed into separately and never shown during the presentation path alongside the original steps' layout. However, the following screenshot shows a zoomed out overview to illustrate how you might utilize the canvas to create seemingly separated content via the use of zooms and paths:

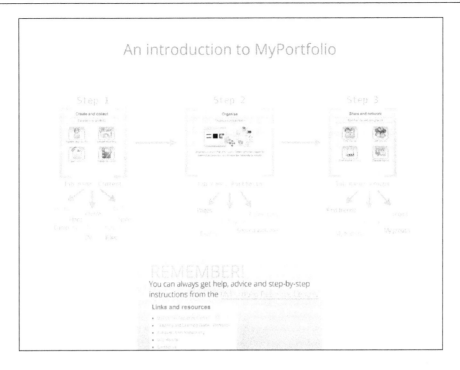

For more advanced design inspirations, you might consider using a contextual background and building up on that with content such as Prezi shapes or stickers to create a scene or staging area for your content to appear. This is hard to describe, but look at the following screenshot and you can see how the background of a building has been used and then layered with cartoon characters that are asking questions:

As the presentation continues, content builds up over the background, using it to determine the layout. Although the background doesn't move, this nonlinear format allows the presenter to build up ideas while keeping the overall context firmly in the audience's mind. This is shown in the following screenshot:

Getting started

Now that you have seen some examples of what can be done, and possibly how you can improve on these examples, it is time to look at what you will need to get started. This book will require a basic understanding of design to allow you to create beautiful presentations. Although you do not need extensive technical knowledge either to utilize Prezi or to understand this book, you will need some familiarity with the technologies referenced in this guide, which are as follows:

- Microsoft PowerPoint
- Prezi
- Adobe Illustrator
- YouTube

Extensive understanding of Prezi is not required, and this book will still cover most of the steps for the purpose of completeness. It is also important to note that while this book will explore how to work with Adobe Illustrator to create great Prezi presentations, it is not itself a guide to Adobe Illustrator.

While the section on themes in this book will look at editing the CSS code within Prezi, it is not expected that you will have previous experience in web or computer programming. The guide will take you through how to make tweaks and will also include some example code for you to experiment with.

Finally, before you can begin to impress both colleagues and clients with your Prezi skills, you will require a few things to get started. These should be things you already have access to and should not cause any additional expense. You will need the following:

- A computer or laptop (with mouse, keyboard, speakers, and ideally a microphone)
- A comfortable space to work
- Some materials to work with (images, videos, and audio files)
- An Internet connection
- Flash version 11.1
- An up-to-date web browser (Internet Explorer, Mozilla Firefox, Google Chrome, and Safari are all compatible)

Please note it is also possible to use a tablet, and if you do use one, you will not need Flash; however, this book will be focusing on using Flash in the use of a more traditional computer/laptop device. If you would like to read more details about Prezi's system requirements, you can do so in the troubleshooting section of their website.

Which account to choose?

When you have all the required hardware and software to begin creating your presentations, you must also set up a Prezi account. You may already have one, and if so, then you can use it. If you do not have one, then you can set one up, and this is quick and easy to do.

Whether you currently do or do not have a Prezi account, it is important to consider which account type to go with. Prezi offers a range of accounts and depending on your usage of the system, different ones will be appropriate. At present, Prezi offers four account types which are shown in the following screenshot:

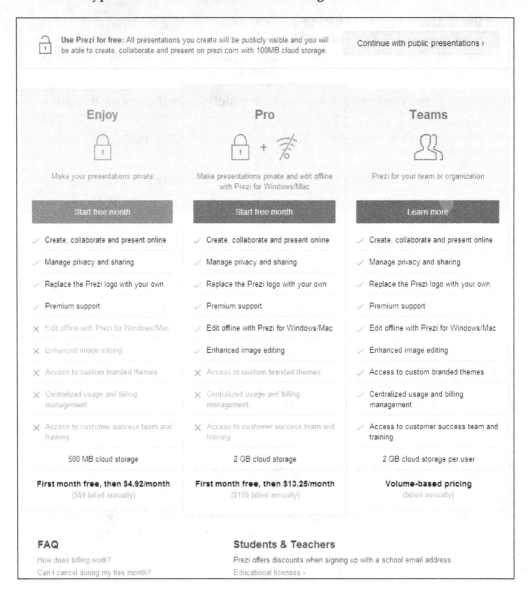

Please note that the prices shown in the previous screenshot were correct at the time of writing in July 2014. If you would like to see more up-to-date prices, please go to the Prezi website pricing section at `http://prezi.com/pricing/`. You may have also noticed at the bottom of the screenshot that there is an additional licensing type, the educational license. Educational licenses are available for a reduced price as **Edu Enjoy**, **Edu Pro**, and **Edu Teams**, but you need an educational e-mail in order to obtain them. Go to the Prezi website at `http://prezi.com/pricing/edu/` for more details.

Moving back to the main account types, you will have noticed from the screenshot that there are four types available: **Public**, **Enjoy**, **Pro**, and **Team** accounts. These have different storage sizes and capabilities, which we will explore in more detail now to see which one is right for you.

It is unlikely that the Public account would be sufficient for extended use as it has a number of drawbacks, including the inability to make presentations private, the Prezi logo on all presentations, and limited (100 MB) storage. However, it can be a good starting point if you are just looking to get an initial idea of how Prezi works as it is a free no-risk account. Once you are happy with the tool, then you may wish to upgrade to one of the paid account types.

The first level of paid account is the Enjoy account. This initial paid level would be suitable for some individuals or smaller firms. It counters the issues of the Public account, including five times more storage (500 MB). Other than combatting the issues of the free account, the Enjoy account offers *premium support*, which means any questions you send to Prezi will be answered within a day.

The Pro account is probably the most suitable for extensive design or business use. Alongside countering the issues of the Public account, the Pro account includes all the features of the Enjoy account. It offers substantially more storage (2 GB) than either of the other accounts. Additionally, the Pro account allows account holders to work offline, which could be valuable if you often find yourself having to work on the move.

You should carefully consider which account type you will need, taking into consideration how much privacy and storage you will use. If you are new to Prezi, it is advisable to start with a lower level account, such as Public or Enjoy, and then you can upgrade if you need additional storage. It is also worth noting that Prezi does offer discounts for multiple licenses, so if you work for a firm and intend on rolling this out to the entire staff, then this could be worth considering.

Summary

This chapter explored the benefits of Prezi and how it differs from traditional tools, predominantly in its ability to allow nonlinear presentation models. We then moved on to get to grips with some of the key terminology for Prezi, which is specific to the system such as frames, paths, and canvas. Next, we looked at some examples to get you inspired and show what is possible. We also highlighted some good designs and looked at how we can do a lot with very little. We then looked at system requirements and finally reviewed the available account types.

Now that you are inspired, have all you need to get started, and have got to grips with the basic terminology, we can move on to some hands-on work. The next chapter will take you through how to work with existing content, including Prezi templates and PowerPoint slides.

2
Working with What You've Got

Getting started with Prezi does not have to take a long time. In fact, it is possible to keep the setup time to a minimum by working solely with the existing content. This chapter will explain how to use the preset Prezi templates to give your presentation a professional feel without having to spend lots of time getting everything just right. It will also show you how, with minimal effort, you can make tweaks to your chosen template to give it your own flair or make it fit your branding color scheme or import your old PowerPoint slides.

The contents of this chapter will take you through the following:

- Introducing templates: Exploring what they might offer
- What can I do with PowerPoint?: An introduction to how you can utilize the existing content
- Creating a Prezi from a template: A practical and hands-on guide to creating a Prezi
- Customizing a Prezi template: Basic guidance on changing the color scheme and styling
- Turning your PowerPoint into a Prezi: Hands-on guidance for converting your slides

Introducing templates

Templates are useful to assist with the transition from linear presentations to a more dynamic format. It can be slightly overwhelming or awkward to get used to, and you might find that, to begin with, a lot of your Prezi presentations may have a fairly linear flow. Don't think that using a template will limit your ability to be creative; they are simply a good time saver. You can still add your own content, tweak the theme, or even rebuild it using the basic elements. The reason we are exploring them is because they are brilliant for when you don't have much time, perhaps due to heavy workload or a last-minute presentation being sprung on you by a client or a colleague.

The templates can help you understand the benefit of a nonlinear style and once you get to grips with it, you might find it to be rather liberating. If you are not so cautious or anxious about moving to a new nonlinear style, then you may find that you end up being rather overenthusiastic about your ability to move in different directions. If this is the case, then it is likely that your first few presentations will induce a slight feeling of motion sickness in your audience. Therefore, the templates can be a useful way of giving yourself a guideline for how to move between frames, even if you completely change the theme and content.

What can I do with PowerPoint?

After looking at adding and customizing templates, the chapter will then move on to demonstrate how you can save even more time by importing existing content from PowerPoint slides. This is a great way to breathe new life into your old presentations, and to show colleagues or clients exactly how Prezi can make the same proven content look even more dynamic and engaging.

When Prezi imports your old PowerPoint presentation, it does this on a slide-by-slide basis, so you can choose how much you want to bring in. You can then deconstruct the elements of each slide you've brought in, as these are all kept separate in Prezi. This means you could update an image on a slide without having to delete the whole thing. This is particularly useful if you do have to change images that are outdated or you do not have the correct licensing permissions.

This chapter will take you through utilizing all of the features mentioned previously in a step-by-step format. It will also mention extra considerations that are specific to when you are setting up a template or importing existing PowerPoint material.

Creating a Prezi from a template

We will start off by creating a Prezi from a template and then move on to look at customizing this template.

As we just discussed, Prezi has a selection of predetermined templates, which have all the formatting, design, and layout already created for you. These templates are easily editable, so they can be used as a starting point, and do allow you to still customize your own design, but we'll get to customization later.

As mentioned in the introduction of this book, Prezi allows you to create a range of presentation styles, meaning you don't have to stick with a nonlinear format. The templates are already set up in a range of styles, and when choosing a template, you should consider which flow would work best for your presentation. The templates can also be useful to demonstrate how different styles might work, so don't be afraid to take some time and experiment with the different flows and get a feel for nonlinear presentations.

Let's start by creating a Prezi from one of the many existing templates:

1. Log in to Prezi and then from the **Your prezis** section, click on the square labeled **New prezi** in the middle of the screen:

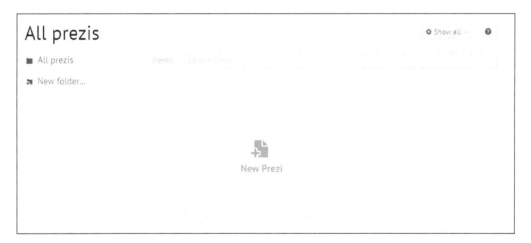

2. A new tab or window will open. Once this has loaded, there should be a window with a list of various templates. These templates also demonstrate different styles of presentations, including **Journey**, **The Big Idea**, and **Explain a Topic**.

3. Click on the **More** button or use the search box to find the template titled **Journey**:

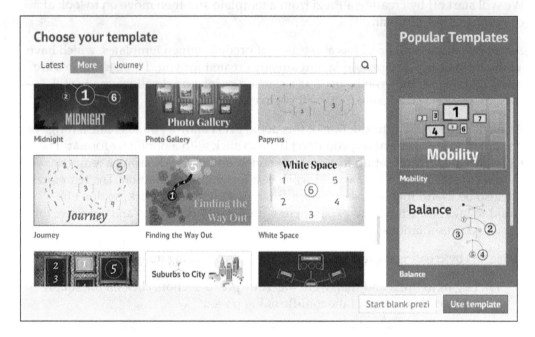

4. When you find this template, either double-click on it or click on the template and then click on the **Use template** button to select it.

5. You will then see the template load into Prezi's editing screen. You will see that it has guidelines built in as to where the title should go, and it will have preplaced frames, which you can fill with content.

6. Click on where it says **Click to add Title**. This is shown in the following screenshot. You will notice that the text disappears and your cursor starts blinking. You can then type into the box. Enter the title, Using a prezi template.

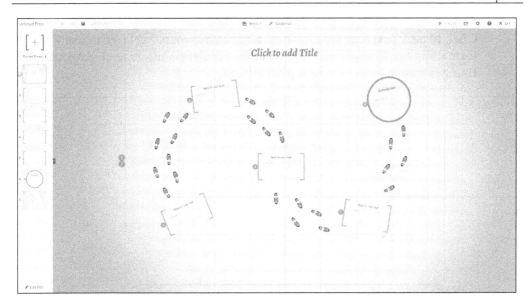

Customizing a Prezi template

Now that we have created our presentation using a Prezi template, we can start to customize the content within it. First, we will look at how to add more text, and we will then move on to look at how to change the color theme.

There are a couple of useful tips to learn before we can start customizing the template. First, if you left-click and hold on any empty area of the screen, you can drag the mouse to move the Prezi around. If you hover your mouse over any of the content, it should get selected with a blue box, and you can then click on **Zoom to Frame** to zoom into it. This is particularly useful when entering text into some of the smaller frames. Now, let's put these tips into practice with the help of the following steps:

1. Using the techniques mentioned earlier, zoom into the first frame on the journey template.

2. You will now be able to see more clearly that there are two predetermined functions. The first, to add a title to the frame, and the second, to allow us to add body text. Click on the first instance where it says **Click to add Text** and enter the title as `Frame Number One`.

3. Once you have entered the title, click on the other instance where it says **Click to add Text** and type in some text of your own. Feel free to use the formatting bar to experiment with adding bullet points as well. An example frame is shown in the following screenshot:

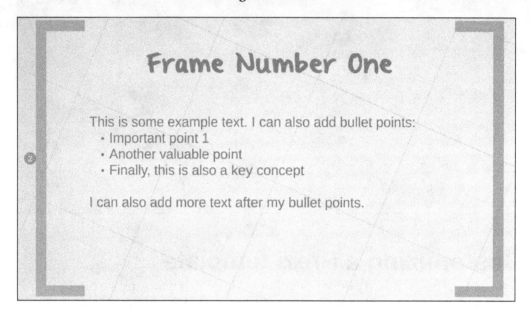

This is some example text. I can also add bullet points:
- Important point 1
- Another valuable point
- Finally, this is also a key concept

I can also add more text after my bullet points.

4. Now zoom back out of the frame by moving your cursor to the middle of the far right edge of the screen. This should produce a vertical grey box with three icons, which have the following appearance; a house, a plus, and a minus. Click on the house to zoom back to the overview of the whole presentation (home). The plus and minus work as zoom in and zoom out respectively:

5. We will now look at changing the color scheme of the template. To do this, go to the button labeled **Customize** in the center of the bar, which runs across the top of the screen, the menu bar.

6. When you click on this button, a drop-down menu will appear containing a number of different themes. Click on one of them to select it and apply it to your template, as shown in the following screenshot:

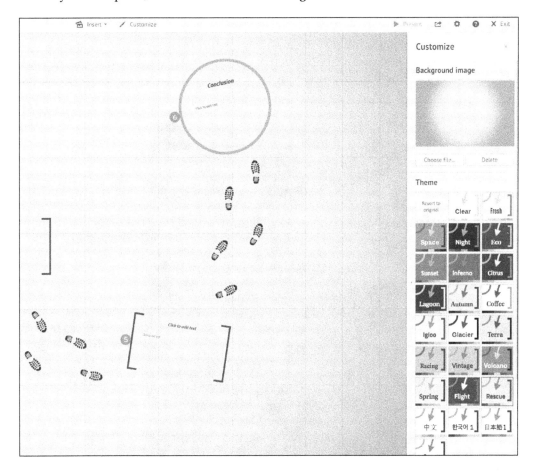

First of all, try selecting one with a vibrant background, such as **Rescue**. You can see that this format works quite nicely with the Journey theme as the yellow contrasts with the footprints, making them stand out more.

Then, see what happens when you try one with a darker background such as **Citrus**. Notice how the footprint elements are harder to see; this is because the background color for that template does not complement the template elements. This is shown in the following screenshot. It is important to bear things like this in mind when customizing your template. As a solution, you could change the background color for the theme or you could delete the conflicting theme element. We will look at customizing themes later in this book, as it is a more advanced skill and would mean the Prezi setup will take a little longer.

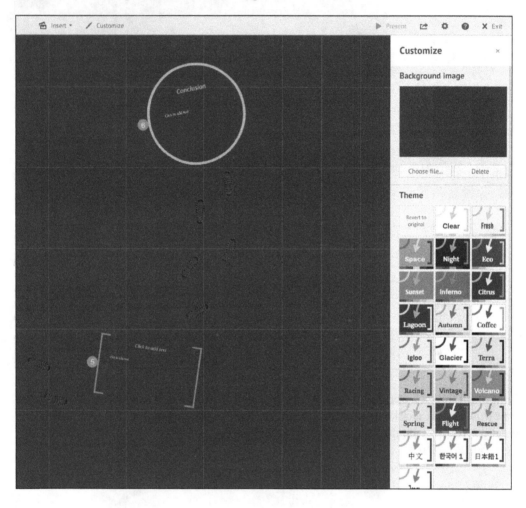

Turning your PowerPoint into a Prezi

Now that we have established how to create a Prezi from a template and how to add text and apply different themes, we can look at how to import our existing content from a PowerPoint presentation. For this section of the chapter, you will need an existing PowerPoint presentation to work with.

When you add your PowerPoint slides to Prezi, it turns each slide into a separate frame. A frame is Prezi's way of grouping together different content, just like PowerPoint groups content by using slides. Once the slide is converted into a frame, Prezi identifies each individual element of content that went into making that slide, such as images, title text, and body text. This means you can still edit and remove these elements individually, just as you would be able to in PowerPoint.

In Prezi, it is easy to have frames within other frames (whereas it is inelegant and clunky to have a slide within a slide when using PowerPoint); this allows you to create subframes. Subframes can be used to hold additional details you are not sure whether you'll have time for. You might also use them to hold notes that you don't need for the main presentation, but that might be useful for colleagues presenting the Prezi or for audience members reviewing the presentation at a later date. You can add a slide as a subframe and simply zoom into it, if you need it, or skip past it, if it's not needed. This is much more subtle than having to skip past the slide in a PowerPoint. We will learn more about this as we develop our Prezi skills.

Without further delay, let's have a go at adding some PowerPoint slides to our Prezi:

1. In the template we have been using for the previous parts of this chapter, locate the **Insert** button (the middle button in the center of the bar that goes across the top of the screen).

2. Click on the **Insert** button and then from the drop-down menu that appears, select **PowerPoint...**, as shown in the following screenshot:

3. You should now be presented with a file explorer window. Use this to navigate to the PowerPoint file you wish to use for this example. When you find the file, click on it and upload it by clicking on **Open**. This file can be any PowerPoint you wish to use but you will also find an example to download at http://digidomi.wordpress.com/2014/08/31/essential-prezi-resources/.

4. This should load the slides into a panel within Prezi, on the right-hand side of the screen.

5. Left-click on the second slide and then drag it onto the Prezi canvas. Release the mouse to drop it somewhere on the screen and then click on the green tick to place it there. This is shown in the following screenshot:

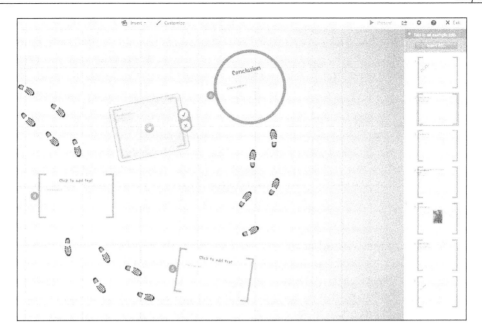

6. Just as we did earlier with the template frames, you can zoom in to it. Do this by clicking on the slide to select it with a blue box, and then click on the **Zoom to Frame** button.

7. You may notice that the slide has become slightly jumbled in the conversion to a Prezi frame. Click on any element of the frame, such as the title or body text, then click and hold the hand icon to drag the content to the desired location:

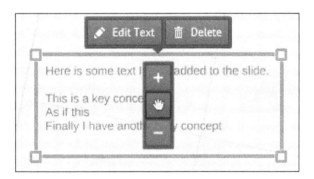

8. You can also use the **Edit Text** button to enter additional text or the dustbin icon to delete the element.

When you are happy, click on the save icon that resembles a floppy disk on the left-hand side of the bar that runs across the top of the screen; this will save your progress. Although Prezi does autosave as you go along, it is always a good idea to do a manual save after making important changes.

Why not try adding some other slides and experiment with how to move and edit the content? It is also a good idea to try dragging one of the slides from the right-hand panel onto the canvas and into an existing template's frame to turn it into a subframe.

Although we have just looked at how to add slides individually, you can insert all the slides from a PowerPoint in just one click. In the side panel that appears when you upload the PowerPoint, instead of dragging the slides one by one, simply click on the button at the top of the panel labeled **Insert All...**. This will then give you a list of layout options and the ability to add a path between them, as shown in the following screenshot. Select the layout you want and tick the path option if desired, and then click on **Insert**. If you do not want any of those layouts, then don't worry, once all of the slides have been placed into the Prezi, you can then move them around by hovering over a slide, and then left-clicking on it and dragging it to your desired location, so just choose any layout.

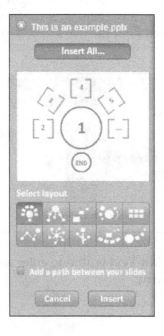

Although you can just add all the slides, it might, however, be useful to go through the slides individually as it can be a good time to review your PowerPoint content and assess what is still useful. This is advisable, rather than simply continuing with the same content, which may no longer be relevant. It is best to only include important information in a Prezi, so narrowing it down is a valuable exercise.

Summary

This chapter has taught us how to create a Prezi presentation using a template, and then how to customize that template. We discussed how changing the color involves being mindful of the styling and elements of the theme we have chosen. We also looked at adding in our existing PowerPoint slides.

We briefly looked at the risks of creating a feeling of motion sickness in the audience, which is a potential pitfall for new users. This is comparable to new users of PowerPoint who feel compelled to overanimate slides by zooming text and animations. Similar to this, motion sickness in Prezi can be eradicated by carefully considering movements around the canvas. Never try to move too far off too sharply. Smaller movements are preferable, and try not to move too jarringly in opposite directions from frame to frame. Ensuring you have a smooth and gentle path through the presentation will mean you are able to enjoy the enormous benefits of Prezi's nonlinear design and customizability.

The next chapter will continue our journey by looking at creating new content; this will present new challenges in its tasks and set you up to use your imagination.

3
Creating Something New

As a creative individual, you are most likely eager to create presentations from scratch, rather than using an existing template. Indeed, there are many benefits to creating a presentation from scratch, including allowing your creativity to flow, being able to showcase your design skills, and being able to naturally fit in your own custom content (such as graphics) without having to force them into a template. It might be that you have no option but to create a presentation from scratch if you are designing for a client rather than for your own personal use. It might also be that there simply isn't a template for your idea. Although Prezi does a good job of offering a template for many types of presentations, it could be that your topic or industry requires a specific design not covered by the templates. You may still wish to browse through the templates for inspiration, but create the presentation from scratch rather than trying to adapt to an existing template.

In this chapter, we will explore a number of considerations to bear in mind when creating a Prezi from scratch. We will also look at practical examples of how to carry out tasks, including adding basic content, moving and adjusting frames, and customizing a theme. The latter section, on how to customize a theme, will build on what we learned about themes in the last chapter and will look at how to edit a theme using CSS code. This will not require prior code knowledge and should be accessible to you, even if you haven't used CSS before, as it will be presented at a basic level. Of course, if you are comfortable with code, then please feel free to use the end of this chapter as a spring board to do more creative customizations.

To summarize, the topics covered in this chapter include:

- Creating a Prezi from scratch
- Adding basic content
- Adjusting frames, rotating, resizing, and moving
- Adding a theme
- Customizing a theme
- Adding 3D backgrounds
- Editing the themes' CSS text

Before you begin

Although much of the other content covered in this chapter is rather simple and shouldn't cause you any great trouble to learn, there are additional considerations you should bear in mind. These include considering the overall impact of any frame adjustments or additions. Consider the impact of a frame rotation on the canvas as a whole, how will it affect the path? This does not mean everything has to be aligned perfectly straight, but consider how moving from a jaunty angle might affect the flow.

We will look at path consideration specifically later in this book, so we won't focus on it too much in this chapter. You should also take into account how changes within frames, such as alignment of text, might affect the presentation. Ask yourself, how does this work with the overall design? These sorts of considerations are particularly relevant when designing a nonlinear presentation as it does open up many options. You could have the frames arranged on the canvas so that you end up working around in a circle, with the canvas completely flipping underside down. This would look unreadable when viewing it outside of a set path (as some frames and their content would be upside down), but within a path might work really naturally, for example, if you had designed the presentation as a spoked wheel, with text going along the spokes, as shown in the following screenshot. This might work well going round as the canvas would flip with the text, as if the wheel were rolling. However, when viewed as a whole, some of the text would be diagonal or upside down, not ideal for reading.

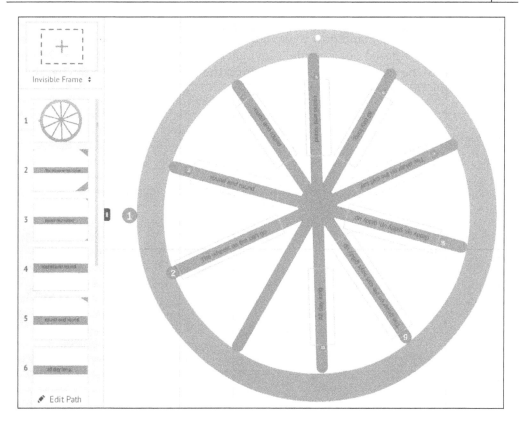

Consider the context of the presentation. Does it call for something formal or informal? Would a movement in a particular direction make more sense? For example, if you are making a reference to sales rates rising, you may wish to have an arrow rise up from one frame to another as the path animates in an upward direction. However, if you were talking about crime rates falling, you may wish to have an arrow animate downwards with the path to the next frame.

It is also valuable to contemplate how you wish the audience to access the presentation when considering what content you might add. If the audience will be guided through the presentation, then you may wish to keep text to a minimum and instead use images as prompts or illustrations for different sections of the presentation. Alternatively, if the presentation is to be accessed remotely by the intended audience in their own time, you may wish to include more text to illustrate points and even consider adding frame-by-frame narration. We will look at adding multimedia content in the next chapter, but it is worth thinking how this might work while constructing a presentation from scratch.

Finally, before we get started with creating our brand new Prezi from scratch, it is essential that you understand how to navigate in the Prezi canvas interface. As you may have already figured out from the previous tasks, the screen has four main areas. These are the central canvas, the panels on the left and right, and the bar that stretches along the top of the screen:

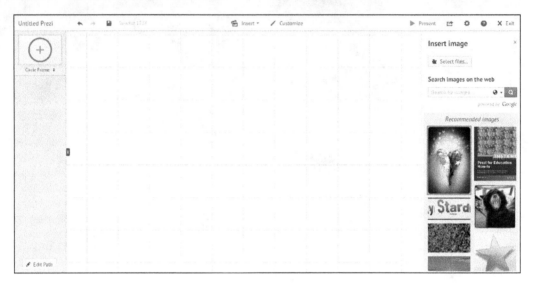

The central canvas is your main creation space, and it therefore has the largest share of the screen. To the left of the screen, you will notice a vertical bar that contains all of the frames as well as the path between them. On the right-hand side of the screen is where you will find contextual panels, such as for inserting images, adding PowerPoint slides, or customizing the theme. In the previous screenshot, the panel is of inserting an image as this was the option selected. You will also find the zoom and home buttons on the right-hand side of the screen. Along the top of the screen is a menu bar, the icons on the left- and right-hand sides of this bar are for administrative functions, such as saving, undo, and printing to PDF. The icons in the center of the top menu bar are used to add different elements to your Prezi.

Now that we have discussed some of the wider elements to consider when constructing a Prezi from scratch, we will get started with a practical task. It is useful if you reflect on what we have discussed so far in this chapter before beginning a new presentation, and try to keep the questions posed (such as how frames will affect the path and how the design works as a whole) in mind while completing the tasks that follow. Our first task will look at setting up a Prezi from scratch.

Creating a Prezi from scratch

This task involves starting a Prezi from scratch, so you can ignore the presentation we created in the previous chapter. We discussed earlier some of the reasons and benefits of starting from scratch, including creativity and flexibility. Without further delay, let's have a go at creating our brand new Prezi. Follow the ensuing steps to set up a Prezi without using any of the templates:

1. Log in to Prezi (`http://prezi.com/`), then from the top-right corner of the **Your prezis** screen, click on the button labeled **New prezi**.

2. A new window should then be launched; this is the same window we saw in the previous chapter for selecting a template. This time, instead of selecting a template in the bottom-right of the pop-up window, click on the **Start blank prezi** button:

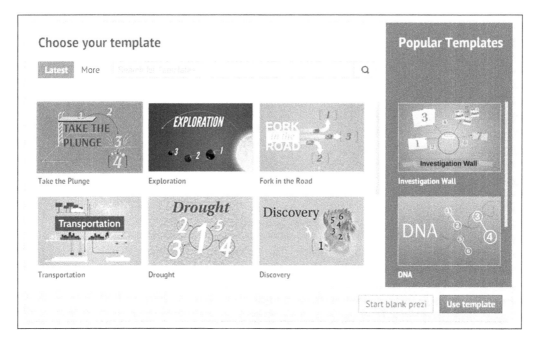

3. When the Prezi loads, you will notice that even though you have requested a blank Prezi, there is a frame already added. You could use this frame as a starting point, but for this task, we will delete it. To do this, click somewhere on the outer line of the frame, then when the option appears, click on the dustbin icon to delete it, as shown in the following screenshot:

You should now have a truly blank canvas. This will allow you to create whatever you want, within some constraints of both the system and your own imagination. To ensure that you add content efficiently and to give yourself a starting point, it is advisable to plan out what you want your presentation to look like first. You may wish to do this on paper or just in your head, depending on how you work best. This will ensure the final presentation is of a higher quality and has a better flow. This advice is of course true even if you are using a template, but when you are creating one from scratch, it is especially useful to think carefully about how you wish to move through the content.

Get a better sense of the canvas space you have to work with by using the plus sign on the right-hand side of the screen to zoom all the way in, or the minus sign to zoom all the way out. You can also zoom with the scroll wheel on your mouse, if you have one. When zooming in or out to the extreme, you will eventually be presented with a message that says you have reached the canvas limit and you can't zoom any further. This is shown in the following screenshot. Be aware of the canvas limits as it is best to avoid being too close to either extremes. Of course, you may also want to start slightly zoomed in depending on how far you wish your presentation to expand or contract.

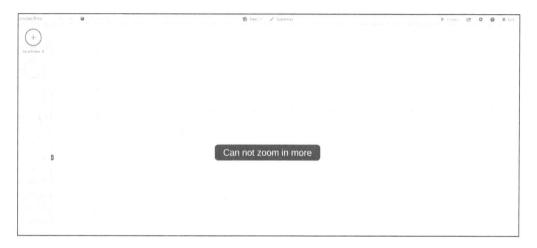

Now that you know what you wish to do with this extensive blank canvas, it is time to take the next steps towards your first masterpiece and start adding content. In this next section, we will look at basic content, but the following chapter will continue to explore more complex content such as custom graphics, multimedia, and external materials.

Adding basic content

There are a number of basic content items you can add to your Prezi, and we will look at all of them in this section. The list includes: text, frames, arrows, lines, highlights, shapes, and symbols.

For adding content, you will almost exclusively need the menu located in the middle of the bar that runs along the top of the screen. The exceptions to this rule of using the top menus include adding text. The titles of the options that run across the top are: **Insert** and **Customize**. **Insert** is a drop-down menu, while **Customize** will launch the themes editing panel:

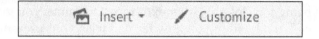

Adding a frame

Let's first look at adding a frame, as this is usually how content will be contained within the frame—just as you would have contained content within a slide in PowerPoint. For this, we will not need to go to the top menus, but instead the left-hand side panel. Along the new frame option is a drop-down menu; you will notice that there are a number of options for adding frames. For the task at hand, we will add a circular frame, but after the task we will discuss the other options. The steps are as follows:

1. In the left-hand side panel, where it says **Rectangle Frame**, click on the two little arrows to expand the drop-down menu.

2. From the list of options, select **Circle**.

3. The menu will then collapse and you will notice that the shape in the preview box above has changed to a circle with a plus inside it.

4. Click on the plus sign in the circle to add your new frame to the canvas. This is shown in the following screenshot:

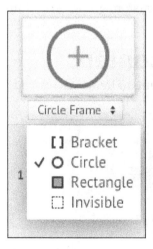

Once you have added your frame, you will want to resize it to suit your needs; we will look at how to manipulate frames slightly later in this chapter. For this example, we created a circular frame as that is the style of frame we have seen in the previous tasks; however, as you may have noticed from the drop-down menu, there are other frame styles available, which are **Bracket**, **Rectangle**, and **Invisible**. All the different frame styles are added in the same way; the only difference is that when adding a bracket frame, for example, the preview will change to a plus sign and bracket. An invisible frame can be useful, as much as the name implies, it allows you to group and contain content within a frame but without having that frame interfere with your design. The frame will be invisible when editing is completed. To allow you to see where the invisible frame has been added during editing, the frame will appear as a faint grey outline, but this will be completely invisible when presenting.

Slightly different to the frame adding option we just looked at is the ability to insert frames which allows you to choose from template frames. This is similar to how PowerPoint allows you to create a new title slide, or slides with a guide area for adding images and text. Adding a frame via the **Insert** menu will present you with a number of circle or bracket frame options. To add a frame in this manner, you must do the following:

1. Click on the **Insert** menu from the top bar to expand it.

2. Select the option marked **Layouts…**.

3. This will launch a panel on the right-hand side of the canvas where you can select your desired template frame:

4. To add one of the template frame options to the Prezi canvas, you will need to double-click on it. Once the frame has loaded into Prezi, you will have the option of replacing any images or text included in the guideline areas.

You may have also noticed a second tab in the **Frames** side panel titled **From Prezis**. This menu will allow you to add frames from previous presentations you have created, making it really easy to reuse something like a contact details frame across multiple presentations.

Adding text

With a frame now added to your Prezi, you will likely want to add some text. Text is a relatively basic thing to want and to add, but it can have a huge impact on your presentation. Unlike the other areas of basic content covered in this chapter, text is not added via the top menu bar. The steps to add text are as follows:

1. To add text, double-click on the area where you wish to add text. This could be within a frame or on the canvas.

2. Where you see the blinking cursor, start entering your text. For this example task, try adding `This is text`.

3. Now, you can edit the text and determine what type of text it is. Using the editing bar that appears above the text you have just entered, select from **Title**, **Subtitle**, and **Body**. This is shown in the following screenshot. The styling of these types of text will vary from theme to theme, and we will look at how to edit them later in the chapter.

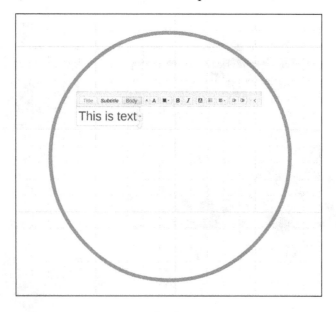

You will also find other editing options in the formatting bar that appears above the text. These include the options to make the text bold or italics, increase the font size, change the font color, add bullet points, and change the alignment.

Highlighting text

It may sometimes be useful to highlight important parts of your text or images. We will look at adding images in the next chapter; so, for now, let's look at how to highlight text. The steps are as follows:

1. From the **Insert** drop-down menu, select **Highlighter**.

2. On the canvas, find the text you just typed and the cursor, which should look like a highlighter pen; left-click and hold while dragging the cursor over the area you wish to highlight.

3. When you are finished highlighting, release the mouse button.

4. The highlighted area is still selectable separately to the text so you can move it or delete it, without affecting the text. This is shown in the following screenshot:

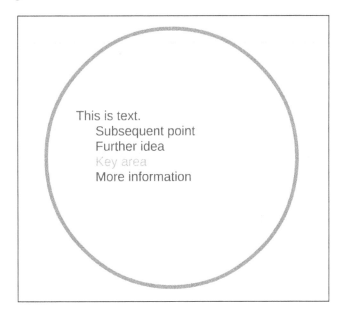

5. To delete, click on the highlighted area and then when this is selected by a blue box, click on the dustbin to delete.

As with the formatting of text styles (title, subtitle, and body), the color of the highlighter can be changed by customizing the theme. Before we move on to look at customizing the theme, we should discuss the other elements of basic content that can be added.

As well as frames, text, and highlighting, which we have just explored, it is also possible to add arrows, lines, shapes, and symbols. All of this content can be added from the **Insert** drop-down menu as shown in the following screenshot, and it is very convenient to have it all available from one well-named option. Although these are all rather simple elements of content, things such as arrows can be really useful in highlighting key concepts or pointing out key ideas. They might also be used as a design feature to map the direction of a path or show movement. Lines can also be used in a similar way. Both of these elements are drawn on to the canvas in the same manner as a frame and can be edited for color and thickness. You can use the multiple editing points to bend or curve an arrow or line.

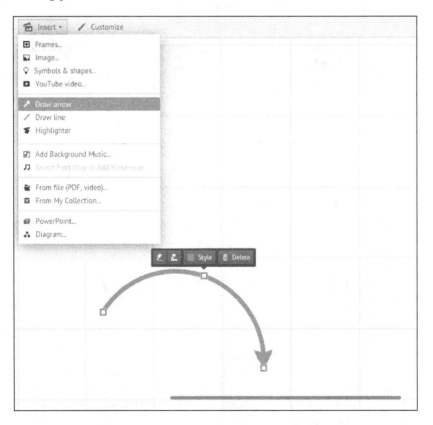

The shapes and symbols, like the rest of the content we have seen so far in this chapter, are added via the **Insert** drop-down menu. The sticker-like symbols are available in a range of styles and include people, objects, thought bubbles, and social media logos. They may be useful for illustrating a point or for adding some flare to your presentation, without having to import external graphics.

The shapes, which are rectangles, circles, and triangles, are available as either outlines or solid shapes. The color of these shapes can be edited once they have been added to the canvas. Both shapes and symbols can be added to the canvas by dragging and dropping them from the right-hand menu where they are displayed. This is shown in the following screenshot:

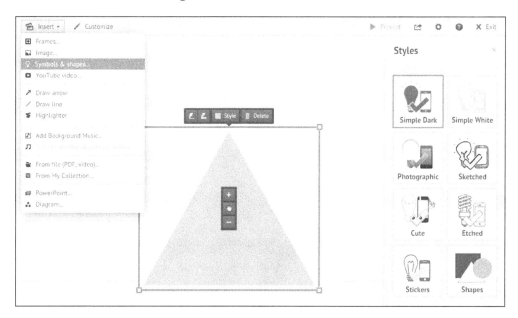

It is fair to say that the basic content in this section is not particularly exciting. As a creative individual, you are probably itching to start getting your own custom graphics into Prezi. However, it is important to ensure you are comfortable with the foundations before we can get more advanced. Often, it is the more basic elements that set off and complement your more complicated multimedia and bespoke content. There are a few more basic areas to cover in this chapter before we can move onto the advanced areas. Next, we will look at adjusting or editing frames and then customizing the theme, which will become slightly more advanced as we look at the CSS code.

Adjusting, rotating, resizing, and moving frames

You have most likely started to get to grips with the concepts of how to manipulate frames and other content in Prezi, as we have completed the previous tasks. You can move content added to the canvas in any direction you want, and the manipulation points are similar to those found in most editing software, including PowerPoint and Adobe Illustrator.

To resize an object, you can either use the plus or minus icons in the center of the item, or you can drag the corners. Both these methods will evenly resize the entire object. If you want to resize just one edge, to make the object wider but not taller, or shorter but not thinner then you can do this by dragging out the relevant edge. This is shown in the following screenshot. This will also allow you to adjust the shape, so you could, for example, turn a rectangle into a square if needed.

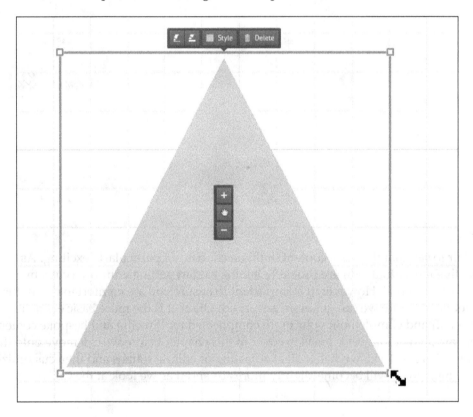

If you want to rotate an object, this can be done by moving the cursor to the corner of the object and then using the mouse to grab the extended manipulation point and dragging it in the direction you wish to rotate. This is illustrated in the following screenshot, and it is a good idea to try it in order to get a sense of what this means:

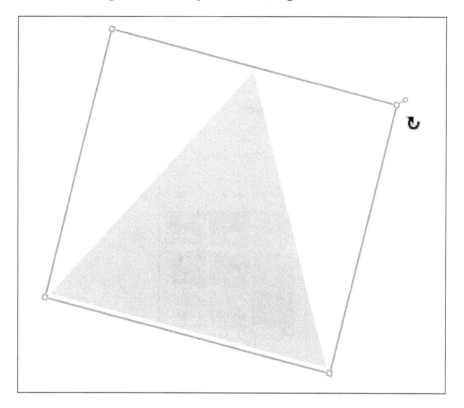

Customizing a theme

Besides the content, another basic task you may wish to carry out is customizing the theme. This section will let you flex your creative muscles a bit by demonstrating how to customize a Prezi theme. In the previous chapter, we looked at how to add a theme; this section provides further explanation on that. The steps are as follows:

1. Click on the button labeled **Customize** in the top menu bar, this will launch the **Customize** panel on the right-hand side:

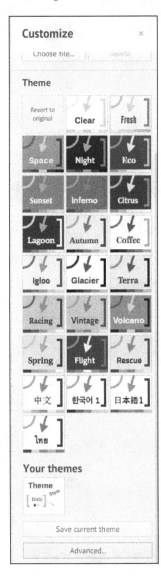

2. Scroll down to the bottom of the side panel and click on **Advanced…**.

3. This should launch the **Theme Wizard**, which will guide you through the editing elements of the theme, including the fonts and colors. Ensure the **Wizard** option is selected in the bottom left of the pop-up window.

4. Change the color of the background and then click on **Next**. We will look at **3D backgrounds** in a separate section after this. Note that in this part of the wizard, you can also add a logo.

5. In the second section of the wizard, you should see an option to edit the theme text, including font styles and colors. Change the font for the title and the color for all three styles. Once you have done this, click on **Next**.

6. The third and final screen of the wizard allows you to edit the color for shapes and frames, as shown in the following screenshot. Using the color picker, change the color for the circle frame as you can see how this affects the preview window.

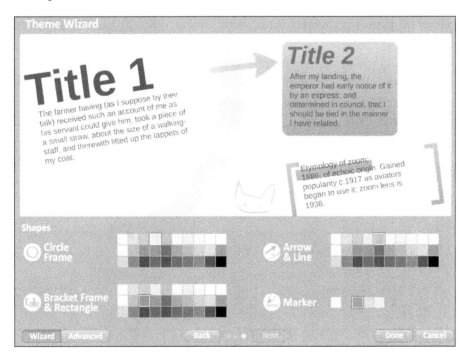

7. When you are happy with the changes, click on **Done** to return to the Prezi canvas.

When customizing the theme as we did in the previous task, it is important to look at the preview at the top of the wizard to see what the theme will look like with your changes applied. Make sure that the colors and fonts you have used work together, and that all the elements are visible (unless you have deliberately done otherwise). If you change the background color, make sure you change all of the lines and frames so that they will stand out against it. Remember that certain color combinations might not work for those with visual impairments, so take this into consideration as well.

3D backgrounds

Having just left the **Theme Wizard**, let's now pop back into it, so we can look at 3D backgrounds. This feature is still labeled as beta, and so it is possible that it could change, but for now, it will work as described in the following steps:

1. Using the **Customize** button on the top menu bar, open the side panel and then click on **Advanced** to launch the **Theme Wizard** as in the task we saw in the previous section.

2. In the bottom left-hand corner of the wizard, there is a button labeled **Advanced**; ensure this is selected and you are in the advanced theme editor.

3. The first option in this new window should be for **3D Background**; click on **Edit** alongside it.

4. A new pop-up window will appear that will allow you to upload up to three different backgrounds; these will be layered in the order you upload them. As you zoom into the canvas, the first background layer will fade into the second and so on.

5. To upload a background layer, click on **Upload** and then browse for your file. Once you have found it, select the file and click on **Open**. A thumbnail preview of the background will then be available in the editor, as shown in the following screenshot:

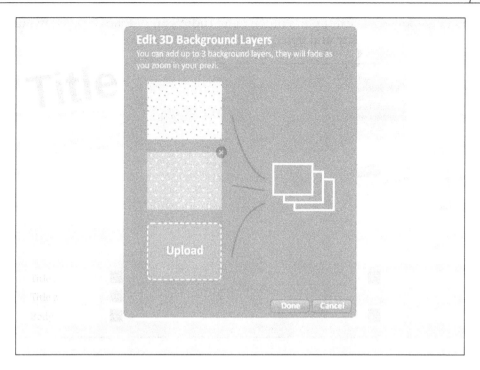

6. Once you have uploaded at least two background images, click on **Done** to return to the wizard, and then click on **Done** again to return to the canvas.

On returning to the canvas, it should become more evident how the layered backgrounds work. Although each one of them will be displayed in full, and separate to the others at certain points along the zoom, they will also fade in and out of one another. The following screenshot shows an example that has been done to be deliberately contrasted, and uses very basic backgrounds. This feature could be used in more dynamic ways, for example, by using the layers to zoom into a human skeleton; the presentation moves in the first layer could be the outside of the human body, the second layer could be a muscular view of the human body, and the third layer could be a human skeleton. There might also be contextual information about each layer as the audience is taken inside the human anatomy.

Although the following example is much more rudimentary than that, it hopefully illustrates the functionality and demonstrates how the fade works gradually.

You might also notice a **3D Background** option on the first screen of the **Wizard** version of the editor, as used in the task for the previous section. This part of the wizard will only allow you to upload a single background, so we are going to ignore it. If you want to upload a single background, you may have discovered this option is available from the top of the **Customize** side panel.

Although the 3D background function opens up many possibilities, it is always important to remember the context and overall design. Consider whether the background is too busy or distracting for the content that will be laid on top of it. Choosing a simple design for the background can add to the overall presentation and even give context or enhance the theme of your design. If used properly, a background can really enhance the overall design of a presentation, but it is not required and many great presentations simply use a solid color background (which includes a *blank* or *white* background).

Editing the themes' CSS code

In this task, we are going to use the CSS code simply to edit the border of a circular frame. This will give you a taste of what can be done by utilizing CSS, and how it can add something extra to your presentation design, without you needing to be a coding genius. The steps are as follows:

1. Click on the **Customize** button in the top menu bar to launch the **Customize** side panel. Then just like the previous two tasks, use the **Advanced** button to open **Theme Wizard**.

2. In the bottom left-hand corner of the wizard, there is a button labeled **Advanced**; ensure this is selected and you will enter the advanced theme editor just as we did in the previous task.

3. In the advanced editor, at the bottom of the window and located in the center, there is a link that says **Use the Prezi CSS Editor**, as shown in the following screenshot. Click on this link to launch the CSS editor.

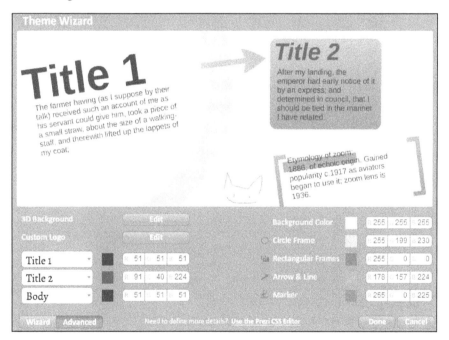

4. After the CSS editor has opened, you can grab it and drag it with your mouse to a more comfortable reading spot on your monitor. It will initially open in the top-right corner of the screen.

5. Draw a circular frame on your canvas, as shown in the following screenshot:

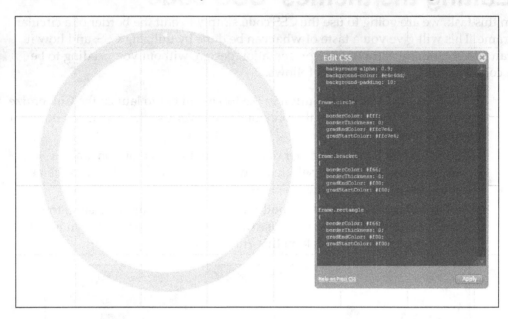

6. Scroll through the code in the CSS editor until you see the code relating to the circle frame; it should look something like the following code snippet:

```
frame.circle
{
    borderColor: #fff;
    borderThickness: 0;
    gradEndColor: #ffc7e6;
    gradStartColor: #ffc7e6;
```

7. Change the values for the borderColor and borderThickness options so that they reflect the following amended code:

```
frame.circle
{
    borderColor: #f66;
    borderThickness: 6;
    gradEndColor: #ffc7e6;
    gradStartColor: #ffc7e6;
```

8. Click on **Apply** and you should see the circle frame you drew change to reflect the amendments you made to the CSS code, as shown in the following screenshot:

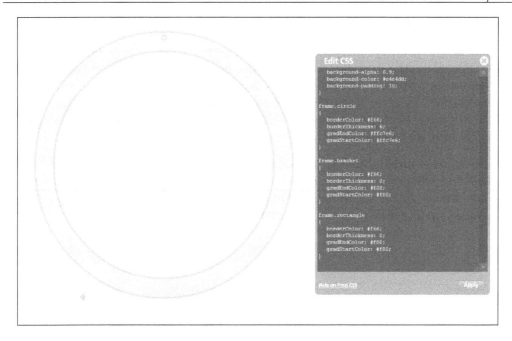

9. To close the CSS editor, simply click on the cross sign in the top-right corner of the window.

This is a basic use of CSS code, but hopefully, it demonstrates how powerful this tool can be for design. A simple tweak such as adding a border to frames can have a big impact on the overall look of a presentation. This sort of customization is not possible through the wizard, and so getting to grips with some basic CSS code can be really useful. If you are already familiar with CSS, then hopefully, this task would have highlighted how valuable it can be to edit CSS code in this manner.

If you are not familiar with CSS, then you might find it useful to use an Internet search engine to look for CSS Color Hex. You will find results that will teach you how to find the correct CSS code, or you can find color pickers that will allow you to pick the color you want and then tell you the code. Sites such as http://www.w3schools.com are particularly useful for this.

Summary

In this chapter, you have learned how to create a Prezi from scratch, rather than using a template. We then moved on to look at how you can fill that presentation with some basic content including frames and text. Once we knew how to utilize these elements, we were able to look at how to manipulate them so they fit in with exactly what we want. The chapter ended by exploring Prezi themes, and we even looked at how we can edit CSS code to get a perfect customization.

By now, your brain might be brimming with ideas on how you can utilize the basic features and functionality covered in this chapter. Let's capitalize on that creativity and take things up a notch by looking at how to bring in your own custom content and embed multimedia into your presentation in the next chapter.

4
Using Existing Content

We have explored most of the tools for creating a presentation and adding Prezi content, and so you are probably quite keen to learn how to add your own content. This chapter will guide you through the myriad of ways you can add your own content and different kinds of content you might want to add. To complete the tasks in this part of the book, you will need to have some content to use. It is also important to ensure it is in the correct file format. The following is a table of the accepted file formats:

Category	Formats
Images	• JPG
	• PNG
	• SWF
Video	• FLV
	• F4V
	• AVI
	• MOV
	• WMV
	• F4V
	• MPG
	• MPEG
	• MP4
	• M4V
	• 3GP

Category	Formats
Audio	• MP3
	• M4A
	• FLAC
	• WMA
	• WAV
	• OGG
	• AAC
	• MP4
	• 3GP
Other files	• PPT (PowerPoint)
	• PDF

Please make sure you have images to practice with in both PNG or JPG and SWF formats as we will look at the SWF files in a separate section.

As you can see from the previous table, there are many types of content you can bring into Prezi; in this chapter, we will look at:

- Uploading images
- Complex graphics (such as layered or vector graphics)
- Multimedia (such as videos)
- Sound files

Finally, we will learn how to embed online-hosted content that is located outside Prezi, such as YouTube videos.

Adding graphics and dynamic content

Adding dynamic content to your presentation is a great idea and certainly something you should always consider. Often, images replace text in a Prezi as the format focuses on visual impact. Presentations in general are not about putting a textbook on a screen, although the level of text included may depend on whether the presentation will be delivered by a presenter or offered to the audience for asynchronous and individual viewing. Images can add to your presentation by serving as decoration or creating aesthetic appeal. They can also serve to add context to a frame or to illustrate a key concept, as can audio and video files. Depending on the topic of the presentation, you may wish to include graphics or multimedia content to demonstrate actual project outcomes; these could be marketing materials or product designs.

There is no harm in recycling content, and it might be that you wish to use a single item, say a graphic, a number of times. An example of where you might want to do this is if you have created a simple graphic, such as a custom arrow. It is reasonable that you would want to use this custom arrow in many locations, and it is unlikely you would wish to upload this graphic each time. Even though uploading content is not a difficult or long process, it would be frustrating to have to keep repeating it. If this is the case, you can save any previously uploaded items to **My Collections**, which will allow you to easily select them again and again. We will look in depth at how to add materials to **My Collections** after we've uploaded our first piece of custom content in the task in the next section.

While uploading your own custom content, and especially while embedding external content, it is always important to bear copyright in mind. This book is not aimed at discussing copyright legislation in different jurisdictions, but it is recommended that you make sure you understand the copyright limitations of the images you are using when uploading and embedding content. Most copyright laws place the burden of responsibility onto the person who uploaded the content. For example, if a client or colleague asks you to upload something you are not familiar with the ownership of, it would be you as the uploader who would face prosecution and not the requester.

It is also worth considering Creative Commons licensing. Creative Commons licensing, often abbreviated to CC, refers to a particular subcategory of content licenses in which an object can be used with permission from its creator who has given copyright permissions to their creative work to certain groups of users, such as educators. An image published under the Creative Commons License is not copyright free, but depending on what you are using it for, you may be able to use it in your own work, copy it, remix it, edit it, or build upon it. CC licenses can come with a number of conditions including attributions (known as *by* licenses), not for commercial use, share-alike, and no derivatives. Before you download and use such images, take the time to find out how Creative Commons licensing works. There is an abundance of information available on the Internet that can be easily found with a web search. Specifically, you may wish to look at Prezi's copyright statement (`http://prezi.com/copyright/`) and the main CC website (`http://creativecommons.org/`).

Adding custom graphics content

This first section will focus on uploading images, so have your PNG or JPG file ready. You can use a simple image as part of your overall design, or use it as a visual marker or evidence for a key concept. In this task, we will look at how to upload an image; how you choose to use it is up to you, and it will surely vary depending on the presentation you are putting together. The key thing to remember, regardless of the nature of the presentation, is to always ask yourself, what does this add? It doesn't have to make or break the presentation but it should always add something, be that decoration or selling an argument. It can also be useful to remember that less can be more. With learning any new tool, it can be tempting to overutilize the new skill you've just acquired, so it is good to play around with adding content before doing your first presentation.

Without further hesitation, let's look at how to add an image to a Prezi presentation. The steps are as follows:

1. Either open an existing Prezi or start a new one.

2. When the Prezi canvas loads, from the top options bar, click on the **Insert** menu to expand it.

3. Click on the **Image...** option in the top section to launch the **Insert image** side panel, as shown in the following screenshot:

4. In this panel, you will see that there are two options for adding an image. You can either upload one or you can search the Web. For this task, we will upload an image, so click on **Select files...**.

5. Browse your computer for the PNG or JPG file you prepared before this task. Once you have found it, select the file and click on **Open**.

6. The image will then load onto the Prezi canvas, as shown in the following screenshot:

7. Once the image has loaded, ensure it is selected. With the image selected, you will notice that there are a number of editing options associated to the image that are not associated to other types of content we have already covered. These new options are **Replace**, **Crop Image**, **Effects**, and **Delete**. They are shown in the following screenshot:

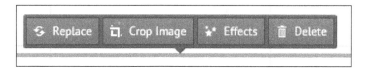

- ○ **Replace**: This option will allow you to easily upload a new image in place of the existing one, without having to reposition it
- ○ **Crop Image**: This option allows you to easily cut out the outside portions of an image that you don't want to display
- ○ **Effects**: This option will enable you to edit the image within the Prezi canvas, which is great if you are short on time and haven't had a chance to load your usual image editing software

Selecting **Effects** will open up the **Photo Editor** window, which has a range of options to allow you to easily and quickly manipulate and enhance your image within Prezi:

The editing options are broken into three categories, each with further options inside them. The top-level options are **Enhance**, **Effects**, and **Frames**:

The **Enhance** option will allow you to play with **Hi-Def**, **Illuminate**, and **Color Fix** options:

You can easily select and unselect these options to see what difference they will make to your images, which will be displayed in a preview window. In the following screenshot, we have added the **Hi-Def** effect to the image to sharpen it up. When you are happy with the changes, you can click on **Apply** to make the changes stick to the image. If after playing, you are not happy with the changes or you don't think they add any value to your image, just click on **Cancel** to return to the higher level of the **Photo Editor** window:

The **Effects** option is a way to experiment with a number of preset image filters, much like you might do in Instagram. It is a quick way to play with images, if you don't have a lot of time or if a professional image editing software is not available to you. Why not try out some of the filters on the image you just uploaded? They might give you some ideas on how you could use them in a future presentation design. As with the **Enhance** option, the effects can be easily applied and removed by clicking on the options. To save any of the applied effects, click on the **Apply** button, and to return to the main **Photo Editor** window without applying any filters, just click on the **Cancel** button. Have a look at the following screenshot:

Finally, the **Frame** option will give you the opportunity to add a frame or border around your image. There is a wide variety of styles available and you might find them to be a nice enhancement to include in your presentation design, as shown in the following screenshot. You could make a feature out of them by theming the presentation as a hallway wall, with a classic style wallpaper as the background. You could then use the photo frames to make your images look as though they are hung on the wall. Open this editing function and scroll through the different options, perhaps you will find inspiration strikes. As with both the previous photo editing tools, you can click on the options to add or remove them from the preview; click on **Apply** to save and on **Cancel** to return to the main **Photo Editor** menu.

When you have finished experimenting with the different photo editing options, and wish to return to the Prezi canvas, click on **Save** if you have made any changes you wish to apply. Or if you have not made changes, or do not wish to save them, click on the cross sign in the top right-hand corner of the **Photo Editor** menu. Please note that clicking on the cross will bring up a warning message to remind you that changes will not be saved. You must then either select **Resume**, to remain in the **Photo Editor** window, **Close** to return to the Prezi canvas without saving changes, or **Save** to apply the changes you have made.

Earlier in this chapter, we mentioned that if you wish to reuse an image, you can save it to **My Collection**. Now that we have uploaded an image, we can look at how this option works. The steps are as follows:

1. Right-click on the image in Prezi to bring up a list of options; these include **Cut**, **Copy**, **Paste**, and **Add to Favorites**:

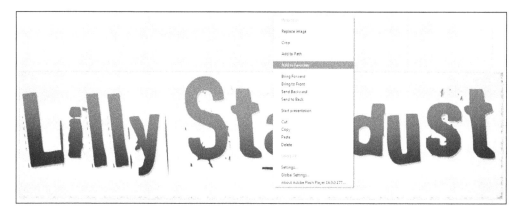

2. Select the **Add to Favorites** option.

It is that straightforward. Once you have saved the image to your collection, you can then access it from the **Insert** menu by choosing the **My Content** option. It is useful to remember that the image will be added to your collection as it is; so if you have applied any effects, these will also be part of the version of the image in your collection.

Adding complex graphics

Depending on what you wish to do with images in Prezi, you may prefer to use complex graphics to get a better quality effect. In this section, we will look at how to add these more complex graphic files, and we will focus on the SWF option, rather than saving complex images as PDFs. Complex graphics include vector graphics and other high quality and layered image files. They have a dynamic pixel count, making them easier to manipulate as the pixels will increase and decrease as you resize, rather than stretching and compressing the same group of pixels, as you would with standard image file types. This means that complex graphics will maintain their integrity regardless of the editing you do to them. Particularly with the zooming feature in Prezi, you may wish to work with complex graphics so that they do not become pixilated as you zoom closer in. You might also find complex graphics easier to work with if you need to manipulate them once they are imported into the canvas, as they will retain their quality. This is something that is important if you wish to show off your design skills to an audience of clients or colleagues.

Adding complex graphics, thankfully, is not a complex task, and is very similar to adding normal graphics; the only difference is you upload it as a file rather than an image. Just to be sure there is no confusion, let's go through uploading a complex graphic together:

1. Using the Prezi you started in the previous task, from the top options bar, click on the **Insert** menu to expand it.

2. Select the **From file (PDF, video)...** option to open the file browser:

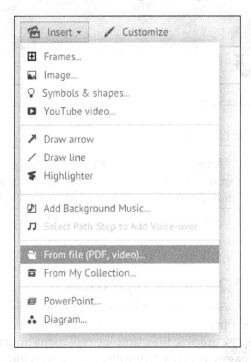

3. Find the SWF file from your computer; once you have located it, select the file and click on **Open**.

4. The complex graphic file will load onto the Prezi canvas.

You will notice that unlike other graphic options, with a SWF or PDF file, you do not get the same editing options. By clicking on the image, you simply get the option to delete. This is shown in the following screenshot:

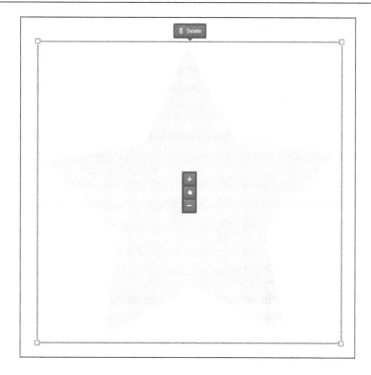

When your file loads into the Prezi canvas, try zooming into it and check the pixel quality. This can be another way of using an image as a background, rather than setting it as background in the theme. You might also wish to use it to load backgrounds for individual frames in Prezi or just to have layers on the theme background to zoom into.

Adding multimedia content

There are a lot of interesting things you can do with images, as the previous two sections have demonstrated. With so many types of media out there, it is not necessary to limit yourself to one type. One of the many brilliant things about Prezi is how easily it allows you to embed multimedia content. Although multimedia files can take many forms, and really only needs to comprise more than one type of media to qualify as multimedia, in this section, we will be focusing on video. When adding multimedia content, such as video, you should carefully consider your audience. A video in a face-to-face presentation can take up valuable time you might wish to use in delivering your argument, and can seem as though you are trying to avoid having to do any work. Of course, if that video is of an appropriate length, succinct, and demonstrates a point well, it could really add value to a face-to-face presentation and might even help aid discussion later on.

With presentations that are intended to be viewed online, a video might help add the dynamism that a face-to-face presentation provides. Consider carefully why you are choosing a video, whether it is an appropriate length, and if it would be better to ask the audience to view it separately either before or after the presentation. Now, let's look at how we can add video to our presentation:

1. You can use the Prezi from the previous task or open a new one.

2. In your open Prezi, from the top options bar, click on the **Insert** menu to expand it.

3. Select the **From file (PDF, video)...** option to open the file browser.

4. Find the video file from your computer, remembering that it must comply with one of the file formats listed for video at the start of the chapter. Select the file and click on **Open**.

5. Once you have opened the file, it may take a few seconds to load into the Prezi canvas; during this time, you will see a **Processing** message on the screen. This should not take too long, but it might vary depending on your current Internet upload speed:

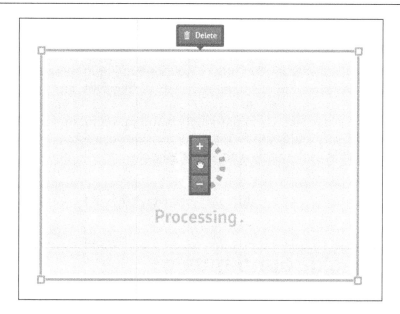

You will notice when your video has been uploaded that, if you ensure it is not selected (with a blue box around it), you can use the play and pause controls to watch the clip within the Prezi canvas. This will work when you are presenting as well, so you can choose whether to play the clip or not and make amendments if you are running over or under time:

Adding sound

Sometimes, visual aesthetics are not the most appropriate direction to take. You may wish to add sound, either instead of other visual content, or to complement it. Again, you should consider your audience, and especially if they have any hearing or visual impairments, which might affect the type of content you add. If an audience member or the whole audience is visually impaired, then adding sound to your Prezi could enhance it dramatically and could be the difference between selling your case and facing a disconnected, perhaps even an alienated audience.

Within Prezi, there are two ways you can add sound to your presentation, either by adding background music or by adding a voiceover. We will look at both methods in this section, but will start with background music.

Adding background music

Background music can be applied to the entire presentation and might be useful for setting a tone to the presentation. Adding a high energy track or something soothing, perhaps some mellow music can affect how people view the visual content in your presentation and change their mindset. This can work for both online and face-to-face presentation delivery. If you are delivering face-to-face presentation with background music, the volume should not be set too loud, so that you can't be heard, or too low, so that the music is lost and has no effect. You should also be cautious when using music with lyrics, as these might distract from any text in the presentation, or from what you are saying. It is both hard to read text or hear speech while it is conflicting with lyrics. Copyright permissions are also an area to be aware of with sound, as they are with other types of media, so make sure you have permission to use your chosen track.

When you have found a song or other audio file you'd like to use as background music, this is how you can add it to your Prezi presentation in a few steps:

1. Working with your existing Prezi, from the top options bar, click on the **Insert** menu to expand it:

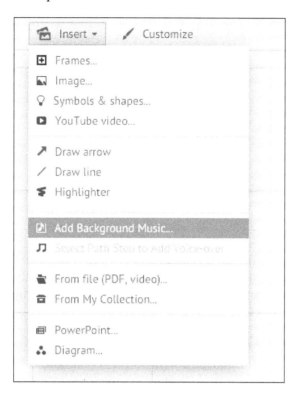

2. Select the **Add Background Music…** option to open a file browser.

3. Using the file explorer, find the audio file that you wish to use. Make sure it has been saved in one of the compatible file types listed in the table at the start of this chapter. When you find the file, select it and click on **Open**.

4. The audio file will then load in the left-hand side panel, underneath the **Edit Path** button. You will briefly see a progress bar, but it should not take long to upload, although this will be dependent on your available Internet upload speeds.

5. If you click on the filename in the side panel, you will see the options to play the file, so you can check whether you have uploaded the right one, and also the option to delete it using the dustbin icon. When you wish to close this pop-up, click on **Done**:

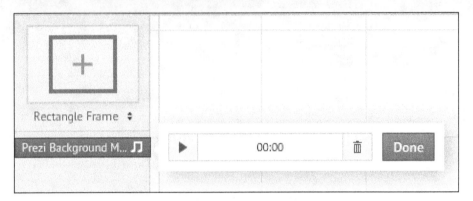

The background music will play automatically and from the start when you begin with your presentation. Bear this in mind when setting your path, so that you can use the music to aid your transitions as you move from one frame or section to the next.

Adding voiceovers

The other way you can utilize an audio file in Prezi is by adding a voiceover. This can be done individually by path step, and hence is quite easy to customize. This would be of particular value if the presentation was viewed remotely or asynchronously and you would not be able to explain the frames otherwise.

There are many freely available or paid-for software packages, which can record audio for you, such as Audacity (`http://audacity.sourceforge.net/`) or Adobe Audition (`https://creative.adobe.com/en/products/audition`). Depending on the quality you want, you could also record on a mobile device, such as a phone if you do not have a microphone. In fact, many mobile phones have fairly decent microphones in them, and you may find them better than a cheap computer microphone. You could also use the voiceover feature to add background music to a single path point, rather than the entire presentation.

The voiceover function will allow you to narrate your presentation and will be added to each or a selected few path points. As you haven't learned about path points yet, you will not have any to add a voiceover to. We will therefore remind ourselves of how to do this when we do look at paths. It is relatively simple to do though. The steps are as follows:

1. Select the path point you wish to add voiceover to and then from the **Insert** menu, select **Add Voice-over to Path Step #1...**:

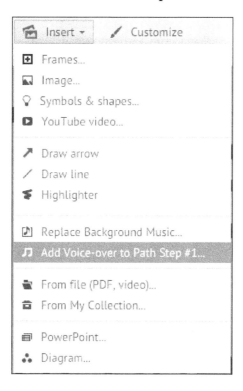

2. This will then launch a file explorer and you can select your pre-recorded voice clip.

3. When the clip has uploaded, you will be able to access it like the background music from the left-hand side panel:

Adding external content

Along with uploading your own custom content, you may wish to embed content already hosted online. This can easily be done for both Google images and YouTube videos. You may wish to pull in your own content this way if you have previously uploaded it. Alternatively, this feature can be useful for pulling in content created by others without having to try to download it while you are unauthorized. We will explore how to add both Google images and YouTube videos in this final section of the chapter.

First, let's look at adding Google images to our presentation. The initial steps are the same as with adding an image, as covered earlier in the chapter, but we will recap them here as well for completeness:

1. Using the same Prezi as for previous tasks, open the **Insert** menu from the top options bar.

2. Click on the first option, **Image...**, to launch the **Insert image** side panel.

3. At the end of the search bar, there is a blue **g** or Google images icon. Click on the drop-down arrow alongside this and then tick the box for **Show only images licensed for commercial use**. This will mean that any images you find during search are completely fine to use in any circumstance. You may wish to use this option even if your presentation isn't for commercial gain, as it will mean you are protected by the images license:

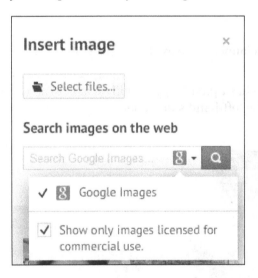

4. Now, use the search box to type in a name or description for an image you wish to find. As an example, try searching for star.

5. Press the *Enter* key or use the blue magnifying glass icon to begin the search.

6. The search should not take long and after a few seconds, a selection of images should appear underneath the search box. You can scroll through these to find the one you like.

7. When you find an image you like, you can either double-click on it or drag it onto the Prezi canvas:

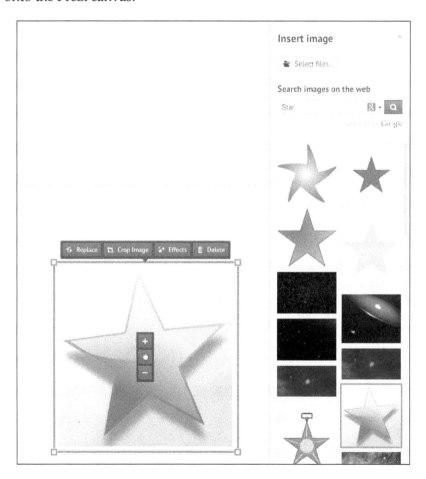

You can edit the image in the same way you would edit an image you have uploaded, using the **Photo Editor** option we discussed earlier in this chapter. The **Insert image** side panel can be closed by clicking the small cross sign in the top right-hand corner of the panel. The easier search function, which allows you to browse images without leaving the Prezi window, makes it convenient to find images for your presentation. The ability to filter by commercial license also means you don't have to worry as much about copyright permissions.

If the content you wish to add is multimedia, for example, a video, then YouTube is a great service. All content uploaded to this service will be covered under *YouTube's terms and conditions*, again meaning you don't have to worry about seeking copyright approval. If the video has been made publicly available to you, then you are free to share it. The only time you might need to check with the owner is if it has been shared with you via a secret link, indicating that the owner is not intending it to be widely circulated.

Another benefit to using a YouTube video with Prezi is that YouTube offers a number of video editing tools when you upload content. This means if you want to use a video you have created, you could upload it to YouTube, make some edits, and then embed it into your presentation. YouTube is a great option if you do not have any editing software available on your computer, or perhaps you are using an unfamiliar computer and want to do everything online. The ability to upload to YouTube from many platforms also makes it an easy way to create video content on a mobile device such as a phone. This content can then be uploaded to YouTube and used in your Prezi presentation. There is no need to transfer large video files, which can be tricky. The following steps will demonstrate how to add YouTube video content to your presentation:

1. With the Prezi you have used for the previous tasks, navigate to the **Insert** menu and expand it.
2. From the drop-down list, select **YouTube video...**, as shown in the following screenshot. This will open the **Insert YouTube** link window.

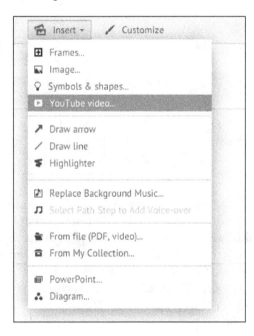

3. Go to YouTube (`http://www.youtube.com`) and find the video you wish to use.

4. Either copy the URL from the address bar or go to the **Share** tab under the video. This is shown in the following screenshot:

5. Return to Prezi and paste the URL into the available space in the **Insert YouTube** link window shown in the following screenshot:

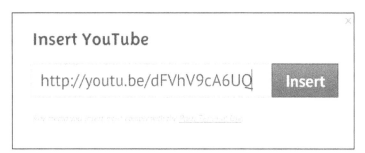

6. Your video will be loaded onto the Prezi canvas. It will have a large play button on top of it. By clicking on the video, you can also access play, pause, and volume controls at the bottom of the video, as shown in the following screenshot:

A useful thing to remember is that if you get the URL from the **Share** tab in YouTube, you can set a start time. This is very useful for ensuring you only include the exact content you need to add value to your presentation. It is a good practice to note down timings of the most useful sections of the video. This way, if you are low on time, you know to go straight to 1:06 and play it until 2:15, for example. Then you only play the most helpful 69 seconds of the video and do not waste time playing the full 10 minutes.

Summary

This chapter allowed us to look at adding a diverse and dynamic range of content. We explored the benefits of a range of media and discussed some points for caution. To begin with, we discovered how to add our own images and the range of files that can be used for this. Moving on, we then looked at moving images, in the form of uploaded video, added directly to Prezi. Next, we talked about how to add audio as either background music or to an individual path step, most likely as a voiceover. Finally, we looked outside of Prezi and discussed some of the ways you can embed external content, such as Google images or YouTube videos.

The next chapter will look at how to work with external packages such as Adobe Illustrator and cover topics such as what file formats to best save them as for use with Prezi.

5
Working with External Packages

This book is focused on how you can easily and most efficiently utilize Prezi to make your presentations more dynamic, more beautiful, and more engaging for your audience. However, as we have been exploring the potential of external content, it would seem irresponsible to not have a brief discussion about some specific and additional considerations when working with external packages, such as Adobe Illustrator.

There are many external software packages you might use to create content, including audio, visual, or multimedia. It would be impractical to consider discussing them all in detail, as this would take up a lot of time, and still might not cover everything. Instead, we will look quite broadly at working with external packages, and then focus on Adobe Illustrator, as this is a very popular graphics package and it is likely you will be using something very similar to this software if you wish to create the vector graphics we discussed in the previous chapter.

In this chapter, we will cover the following topics:

- What file formats to use
- Working with Adobe Illustrator

This chapter is only covering Adobe Illustrator as it felt important to give a concrete example of using a graphics program and translating those files to Prezi. However, to look into all of the possible software packages that might be used would be time-consuming. Adobe Illustrator was selected as it is very popular, as is the entire Adobe Creative Suite; the software will have similar interfaces. If you need guidance on a specific program, then please see the online library of Packt Publishing at https://www.packtpub.com/all/?search=graphics#.

Creating the content

When creating your content, whatever type of media it is, you should consider how it will fit with your presentation. Does it use the same color palette? It is important to make sure it won't look out of place when you import it, as this would make all your efforts to create something beautiful go to waste. It is not just complete clashes you should be aware of; sometimes, near matches can be just as bad. Like a visible jump-cut in a video, if you have a background color for the presentation that is a shade or two different from the background color of a custom image, it will stand out and may not have the effect you intended. This is shown in the following screenshot. Be sure to get the RGB levels (Red, Green, and Blue color model), or whichever color scale you wish to use right. Prezi uses the RGB color model, which is based on the principle of mixing red, green, and blue (all additive primary colors); you can recreate a wide variety of other colors. You can also use the color palate in Prezi, or you can use CSS as we explored in the last chapter and insert the correct color hex.

Along with color, you should also consider the style of the content, and whether this fits the theme you have chosen for your Prezi. For example, if you are using the sketch style in Prezi, then you would want any graphics over a video clip, such as text, graphics, and illustration, to match this style.

This may be out of your control if you are using content you have not produced, but if you wish to show off content of your own creation, it is worth keeping in mind.

The final thought to be conscious of when initially creating your media is shape. This might sound unusual, but consider this: if your Prezi presentation uses all circular frames, and you import a square image, how will this look? Could you make the image circular as well? Should you consider balancing out the Prezi with a square font, or some different shapes? There is not necessarily a right or wrong answer, as it will depend on the media you are creating and the purpose of the presentation. But it is helpful to ensure you have considered this when building the presentation. Just as your content can complement or enhance the background and theme of your Prezi, so too can the reverse be true. If you bear this in mind, you should have a harmonious presentation at the end, which is both eye-catching and informative.

File size

Once you have completed the creation of your beautiful media content, you then need to think about the file it will become. It is essential to consider both the file size and the file type. File size is a more flexible area, as your overall storage limit in Prezi will depend on the license you have. We looked at the licenses in the first chapter of this book, but to recap, the storage limits are as follows:

License type	Storage limit
Public (free)	100 MB
Enjoy ($4.92/month)	500 MB
Edu Enjoy (free)	500 MB
Pro ($13.25/ month)	2 GB
Edu Pro ($4.92/ month)	2 GB

 Please note that these prices are correct at the time of writing this and may have changed since, but they should still offer a guideline.

The more you pay, the more space you get—which is why it is worth considering the size of your files before uploading them. Also, remember that the Edu licenses are only available to those working in the Education sector, or studying.

That covers overall storage; as for the limit per upload, there is nothing in terms of bit size allowance for images. However, there is a pixel limit as the maximum size for any image is 2880 x 2880 pixels, unless it's inserted as a 3D background image. For video uploads, there is a bit size limit, but it varies depending on your licensing type. According to Prezi's own help pages, for Public, Enjoy, and Edu Enjoy users, the limit is 50 MB. While for Pro and Edu Pro users, the only limit is the online storage space provided by their accounts.

Regardless of the license type you have for Prezi, another fact to bear in mind when considering file size is your connection speeds. This book is focused on the online version of Prezi, and when using any online tool, you need to consider the speed of your Internet connection for both uploading and downloading content, as this will affect performance. For example, you may find uploading a larger file fast and simple at work; however, if you have to work out of the office, you may find Wi-Fi connections much slower.

A desktop version of Prezi is available as an application for both Mac (`http://prezi.com/mac/`) and Windows (`http://prezi.com/windows/`), and this will erase your dependency on Internet speed. However, it is worth noting that you would then need to make sure the presentation is synced with your online account before you can edit it from another location. The tool will work the same if it is online or a desktop app, so consider what has the most benefit to your working situation.

File types

Now that we know we want to constrain the size of our files, one of the best ways to do this can be through the file type. Some file types will produce larger files than others, and this is mostly down to the number and type of pixels they use to compile the file. It is also important to learn that size is not everything. In the previous chapter, we looked at the accepted file types. What file type you work with depends on the results you want and the quality required. Remember, larger files will take more time to upload but may also be of a better quality. Let's use this section to discuss the different available file types for images, as we have been working mostly with this media. Of course, there are also quality and compression issues connected with the file types of audio, video, and multimedia content, but as there is a wider range of file types accepted in this area, we will not go into them here.

To remind ourselves, the available file types for image files are JPG, PNG, and SWF—although SWF graphics are uploaded as files and not as images. Out of these three file types, JPG has the lowest quality. It will work for many files where pixel density is not required to be high, and also may be the most commonly available file type when acquiring images from other sources. Moving up the quality scale, PNG files are better than JPG and good for using on the Web as they often offer a more compressed file.

Finally, as we briefly explored in the previous chapter, SWF files are great for complex graphics, especially if working with a professional editing software. However, it is worth bearing in mind that this format cannot be edited. Therefore, it may be worth saving any document created using an editing tool in both its editable file format, and in a format that will be appropriate for upload. For example, you could save the image as an `.ai` file in Adobe Illustrator so that you can later make adjustments using the separate layers you may have created, and you can also compress the layers and reduce the file size by saving it as a `.swf` or `.png` file for uploading to the Web.

Balancing the need for quality, file types, and file size can be a delicate exercise and is a likely one you will improve at, over time and with experience. Your previous experience of working with certain types of files, or creating content for the Web will also influence how quickly you master this skill when utilizing Prezi.

Working with Adobe Illustrator

To make this discussion more concrete, let's look at an example of saving a file created in Adobe Illustrator so that it can be easily edited and uploaded to Prezi as a vector graphic, maintaining its dynamic pixels. The steps are as follows:

1. Open Adobe Illustrator and quickly create a simple vector graphic, something basic such as a star, but utilizing dynamic pixels so that it could endlessly be zoomed in to without losing quality:

2. Save this image as a `.ai` file by expanding the **File** drop-down menu in the top left-hand corner of the screen. Next, you need to select **Save As...**, as shown in the following screenshot. Then, when the file browser window pops up, navigate to the folder or location you wish to save the file to and ensure **Adobe Illustrator (*.AI)** is selected from the **Save as type** drop-down menu:

3. Now, we need to export the image to a `.swf` file. This can be done again using the **File** drop-down menu in the top left-hand corner of the screen, but this time you should select **Export...**. Once the file browser window pops up, make sure you are saving to the destination you require and have chosen an appropriate filename. You also need to select **Flash (*.SWF)** from the **Save as type** drop-down menu:

That is all you have to do to ensure your vector graphics will work with your Prezi presentation. Remember the `.ai` file can be changed and edited, whereas the `.swf` file cannot. This means if you want to make any changes, you would need to make them in the `.ai` file, save these changes, and then re-export the image as a `.swf` type. You would then need to reupload the new `.swf` file to Prezi, using it to replace the previous image.

It is also worth highlighting that `.swf` is a Flash-based file format and so may not be compatible on all devices. Having said that, Prezi also uses Flash and so it too might not work well on certain devices. This is why they have developed the Prezi Presenter app for iPads and iPhones, where you can view but not edit presentations. You can find out more about the apps via the Prezi website at `http://prezi.com/ipad/` for the iPad and at `http://prezi.com/iphone/` for the iPhone.

A similar process can also be done with other editing tools, and there are a number of useful guides on using such tools from Packt Publishing. You could try searching the Web for guidance on saving in certain file formats using specific tools.

Summary

This chapter has discussed the file types that are appropriate for the Web, and how you may still wish to maintain copies of files in original formats, which are larger but contain more information to allow you to make adjustments. We have also explored the other ways you can use Prezi, both on a computer desktop and via the iOS apps. Additionally, we looked at how to prepare files in Adobe Illustrator and then convert them so they can be used in Prezi, without losing any quality.

Now that we have learned how to create and utilize content in Prezi, the next chapter will look at pulling everything together to perfect the presentation with timings and transitions.

6
Making it Work Together

In the previous chapters, we looked at how to create and import content in Prezi. This included adding text, frames, shapes, and media—all of which add value to your presentation. At this stage, although you will have a range of fantastic content, it may lack structure. There is currently no way to easily move through your presentation like PowerPoint does, allowing you to skip from slide to slide with the click of a button. This chapter will look at how you can bring all of your content together, as well as making everything work seamlessly. There are many ways Prezi can facilitate this, including allowing you to group content for editing. Another important feature is the ability to add paths, which creates a flow and direction through your presentation. You can add extra details such as audio to your path, animations within a path point, and timings as finishing touches.

To summarize, this chapter will cover the following topics:

- Grouping content
- Creating paths
- Adding timings
- Adding animations to your path

Grouping content

You may wish to resize, move, or rotate a number of items in your presentation at the same time, especially if you want them to stay scaled or remain aligned. This can be done in a number of ways, either by using frames or by grouping content. Earlier in this book, we looked at using frames and they are a way to contain content as you would normally group it on a slide in PowerPoint. If you manipulate a frame by moving it, resizing it, or rotating it, then this action will apply to any content in the frame as well. This transformation will occur without losing aspects such as proportion between items or alignment; for example, if you have the title larger than the body text, this will remain so, even as you increase the size of both.

A frame will group content to a certain extent, but this is not the only way to group content together. You can also group content outside of a frame, by selecting the element you want to lock together. There are a couple of ways you can do this and many reasons why you might want to. We will explore some of the reasons and uses as we look at how to group for editing and how to group creatively.

Grouping for editing

If you have content that is not contained within a frame, or perhaps occurs in a couple of different frames, you can group it to make editing easier. In the following screenshot, we will look at grouping two frames together, so that they can be easily manipulated while maintaining their relativity:

1. Select the first frame, then hold down the *Shift* key and select the second frame.

2. You should now see a single blue box highlighting both of the frames. Click on the **Group** button which appears above both the frames:

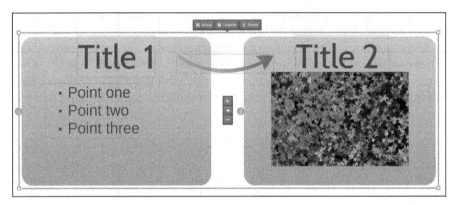

3. You should now be able to transform both the frames at the same time. If you wish to make an independent change to one frame, you must break the grouping. This can be done by clicking on the grouped selection and then clicking on **Ungroup**:

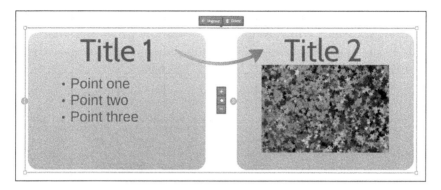

Grouping creatively

There are many administrative reasons why grouping content is useful, but there are also a number of more fun ways to utilize this feature. A creative use of grouping might be to combine basic shapes to create a new shape. Let's try using five different triangles to make a star. We can then group these individual shapes and keep that grouping so that we can manipulate and utilize the star shape as a single object. This next task will utilize what we learned about the creation and manipulation of shapes in *Chapter 3*, *Creating Something New*; refer to this chapter if you need a refresher on how to add a shape or edit the size or color. Without further delay, let's begin. The steps are as follows:

1. Using the **Insert** menu, add a triangle to the canvas.

2. Once you have a triangle on the canvas, you need to duplicate this four times. Either copy and paste the shape or add it to your favorites and use it to replicate the size. You may wish to change the color of each of the triangles for clarity during the construction stage:

3. Arrange the triangles so that they form the shape of a star. To make the illustration easier for this example, you will notice that each triangle is a different color; this is simply to highlight the placement of each shape during construction:

4. Make any tweaks or re-size the individual triangles if required and; ensure that all of the triangles are of the same color if you changed it earlier:

5. When you are happy with the overall shape of the star, you can group it. Rather than individually selecting each of the triangles, left-click on the mouse and hold the *Shift* key, and then drag the cursor across the star, so that all triangles are selected; now, release the mouse. To get a better view of what you're doing, scroll to zoom into the shape:

6. With all of the shapes selected, click on the **Group** option to connect them as one shape:

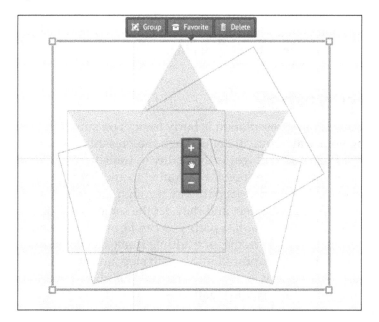

7. You can now transform the star as a single object, including deletion in one click. If you wish to break the grouping of the triangles, either to make alterations to their individual shape or to change the color, then click on **Ungroup**:

Whether this is enabling you to create something or just for easy editing, the ability to group content opens a lot of possibilities. It can be permanent or temporary depending on your needs, which opens up the ways in which you can use it. Grouping is particularly helpful to maintain the original relationship between elements when moving the grouping around. This means that by using grouping, you can move an item, while ensuring you maintain the distance you have set between it and any other item in the grouping.

Creating paths

The flow of a PowerPoint presentation is fairly basic. You simply move from slide to slide, making your way sequentially through the presentation. As we have already discussed, one of Prezi's advantages is the ability to transition in a nonlinear way. This transition from one section (possibly a frame) to another is called the **path**, and as you might guess, it is your pre-set pathway through the presentation. Each of the steps on a path is called a path step, and they act the same as a slide in a PowerPoint presentation. Unlike a slide though, a path step can be anywhere on the canvas and can contain no frames, a single frame, or multiple frames. Content does not have to be grouped in any way to be captured into a path step, and there is a function to simply capture your current view of the canvas. This allows you to move from a wide shot of the entire canvas into smaller sections and then to zoom back out for a wider shot of a particular section or the whole canvas.

The larger the distance between two objects and the more different their positions on the canvas, the larger the zoom will be between the path steps and the more nauseating it will be for the viewer to watch. Be conservative in your use of zooms — remember, users may not be used to watching 3D style presentations.

Each path step will have a number progressing in consecutive sequence, from one up to however many steps you have. The step numbers will help you see the pathway through your presentation quickly and clearly; for instance, if you are adding more steps, and you wish to see where you have come from or just want to review them by glancing at the canvas.

As indicated earlier, there are two ways to create a new path step, either by adding a particular element of the canvas or by adding your current view. We will look at both of these options, starting with adding by selection.

Adding by selection

Adding by selection allows you to precisely choose the frame or content you want to move to next in the presentation. It is the best option if you want a path step to show detail or focus, especially if you want it zoomed in tightly on the content. The following steps will demonstrate how to add a path step in this manner:

1. In the left-hand panel at the bottom, click on the button labeled **Edit Path**.

2. Using the mouse cursor, select the frame or other element you would like to add as a path step. As you hover your cursor over the desired section, you will notice a number in a circle appear; this will indicate the step number and helps show which previous step it came from, as shown in the following screenshot:

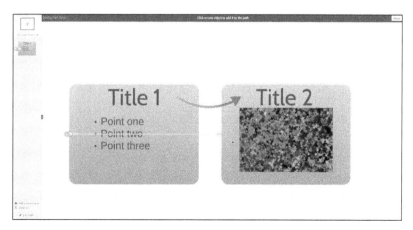

3. Once you have selected the frame or content you wish to add as a path step, click on **Done** to save this addition (you will find the **Done** button in the top right-hand corner of the screen, as shown in the previous screenshot.) The canvas will then look like the following screenshot:

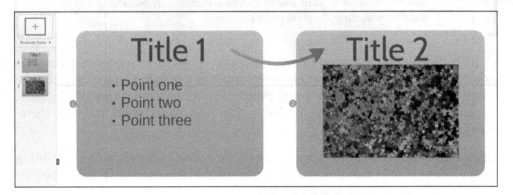

When you have added a new path step, you will notice it appears as part of the list of steps in the panel to the left of the canvas. You will also notice the step number appears next to the frame or content in the Prezi canvas, even when you do not have path editing turned on. This is like the slide sorter view in PowerPoint.

Adding by current view

Adding content by selection is useful when you want to be specific, but not great for those wide shots that show an overview of the canvas, or if you want to highlight multiple frames simultaneously. For more general selection of the canvas, you can add a path step using the current view option. The steps are as follows:

1. Just as in the previous task, in the panel on the left of the canvas, click on the button labeled **Edit Path**.

2. This should make additional buttons appear in the bottom of the panel. Click on the button marked **Add current view**:

3. Whatever is currently displayed on the screen will be added as a path step. A box will appear around the added content, along with the relevant step number, as shown in the following screenshot:

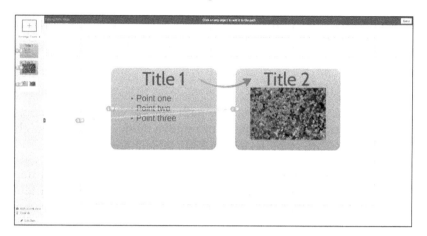

 If your current view is a close-up, that is exactly what will be displayed as the next step, and vice versa. Scroll in and out until you are comfortable with the view you want displayed.

4. If you are happy with this addition, click on **Done** (in the top-right corner) to confirm.

5. You will again see that this selection can be seen even when you are no longer in the **Edit Path** mode. The canvas is shown in the following screenshot:

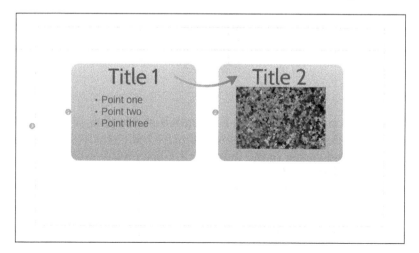

When you are done adding path steps, click on **Edit Path** to close the step adding too, otherwise you will find yourself adding new steps each time you try to adjust the canvas. As this method of creating a step will add the current view of the Prezi canvas, ensure it is lined up and zoomed in as desired before adding it. It is also worth noting that the snapshot Prezi takes for this method tends to be slightly tighter than the actual size of the canvas displayed, so it is worth leaving some room around the edges.

Editing the path

After you have spent some time adding new path steps to your presentation, it is likely that you may at some stage wish to amend or remove them. It is fairly straightforward to rearrange and delete path steps, so let's quickly look at how this is done.

To rearrange the order of the path steps, for example, moving the current step **3** to the top of the list so it becomes step **1**, you must first click on **Edit Path**. Then, simply drag and drop the thumbnails in the left-hand panel to adjust the order, as demonstrated in the following screenshot:

To delete a step, you must also click on **Edit Path** first. Then, hover the mouse over the step you wish to delete, and you should notice a red circle with a cross appear over the top right-hand corner of the thumbnail. Click on this cross sign to delete the step from the presentation path:

With the path editing turned on, you will also notice a **Clear all** option located at the bottom of the left-hand panel; use this if you wish to start the path again from scratch.

In *Chapter 4, Using Existing Content*, we looked at adding audio to a path step, perhaps in the form of a voiceover clip. Hopefully, now that we have explored the concept of Prezi paths in more detail, this will make more sense to you. To recap how this is added, please review the section on audio in *Chapter 4, Using Existing Content*.

Adding animations to your path

Along with controlling the pathway through your presentation, you may also wish to determine an order for content to appear within a path step. You can do this by adding animations to your path, which work much like animations in PowerPoint. In Prezi, animations can only be set to allow for content to fade in, but it is a nice way of building content without having to zoom around the canvas, which could risk making the audience feel motion sick.

The following steps will show you how to add animations, but first you will need to ensure you have created a path to add the animation to:

1. In the bottom of the panel to the left of the canvas, click on **Edit Path**.

2. Select the path step you wish to add animations to, as shown in the following screenshot:

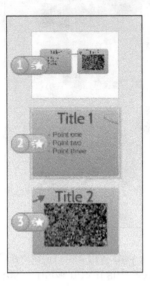

3. Click on the star icon that appears next to the path step number.

4. Select, in order, the element of contents within that path step that you wish to animate. You will notice that these become numbered:

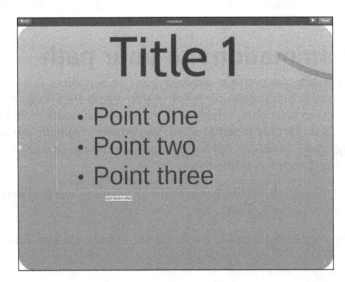

5. You can use the play button at the top right of the **Animation** screen to preview the path animations.

6. When you are happy, click on **Done**.

Once you leave the **Animation** screen, you will notice that the path step in the left-hand side panel now has a star icon on it; it indicates that it has been animated. You can see this in the following screenshot. Notice how path step **2** is different from the others.

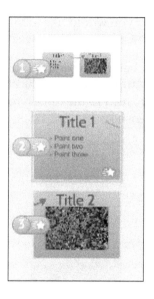

As a creative use of this feature, why not try layering content and animating in the top layer of content. For example, you could have a frowning face and then place a happy face on top of it to show a change in emotion or as an illustration while you give a bad example of practice and then a good example, for instance. In the normal Prezi canvas, only the happy face would show, but you could animate the happy face to fade in. This would mean when you are presenting, the frowning face would be seen on the Prezi canvas, and then the happy face would replace it, perhaps indicating how people's mood will improve after seeing your presentation. For the rest of the presentation, the happy face would be the only one visible on the canvas. This is a nice way to change the content without having to move around the canvas, and really utilize the space.

Adding timings

The final topic we will explore in this chapter is adding timings. Although it is not possible to add timings to each individual path step, you can use the **Autoplay** function when presenting to determine how long each step will be on the screen. The interval time will be the same for all steps, so consider it carefully before setting. The available options are intervals of **4**, **10**, or **20** seconds between path steps. This means that Prezi lends itself nicely to the PechaKucha style of presentation, as you can easily set your 20 paths' steps to 20 second intervals without a need for any additional time keeping apparatus, such as a stopwatch. If you would like to find out more about this style of presentation, you can read about it at http://en.wikipedia.org/wiki/PechaKucha.

Timings are added immediately before presenting, rather than in the editing view we have been working with. The **Autoplay** option is located in the bottom right-hand corner of the presentation screen, next to the option for fullscreen. You will find this illustrated in the following screenshot:

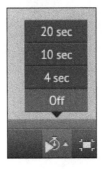

Simply click to expand the menu and then choose the required interval or select **Off** to disable the feature.

Summary

In this chapter, we looked at how to make content work together. This led to a discussion on how to utilize the grouping of content, for both administrative and creative ends. To demonstrate this, we experimented with using triangles to build our own star shape, which with grouping could be manipulated as a single shape. We then moved on to look at paths, exploring how best to establish a preset route through our presentation moving either between frames, areas of content, or individual items. From here, we were able to expand upon paths to look at adding animations to our individual path steps. These allowed us to build up layers of content in a path step, which could be useful for reducing the amount we have to move around the canvas. Finally, we looked at how we can set timings, perfect for delivering a PechaKucha or elevator-pitch-styled presentation.

In the next chapter, we will move on from adding and manipulating our content, as we have covered previously, and instead look at how we can collaborate. Working together is often important and Prezi allows you to share your presentation easily and even invite collaborates to work on a Prezi simultaneously. This means that time or distance need not prevent excellent teamwork.

7
Collaborating

Now that we have explored the numerous ways you can add and create content in Prezi, let's spend some time looking at what else you can use the tool for. Creating a presentation often isn't a solo endeavor; whether you are working with co-authors or need to seek a client or colleague's approval, the ability to collaborate is highly desirable. In this final chapter, we will explore how you can invite others to edit your Prezi presentation and then work together to edit it as a group in real time. We will also discuss how you might share your presentation, for both viewing and reuse purposes.

This chapter will cover the following key areas:

- Sharing
- Inviting editors
- Editing as a group

Inviting editors

If you are working on a presentation as a team, then you will likely want to invite others to assist you with the editing. This might be because you are the designer and someone else is handling the content (or vice versa), or it could be because you are working collaboratively, sharing the required tasks. In this section, we will look at how you can invite a colleague, co-editor, or team of people to edit your Prezi presentation.

In the following steps, we will look at how you can easily add one editor, although the steps can be amended to add other people at the same time:

1. From the Prezi screen, click on the title of the presentation you wish to add an editor to:

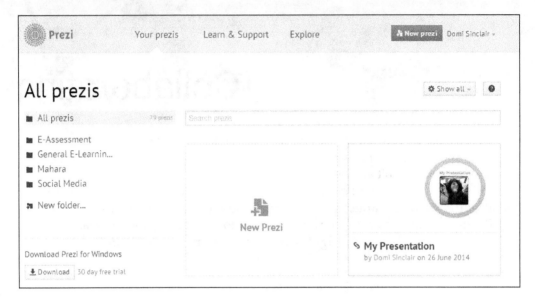

2. Under the preview of the presentation, click on the button labeled **Share**.

3. This will open a pop-up window. At the bottom of the new window, type in the e-mail address of the person you wish to add as an editor:

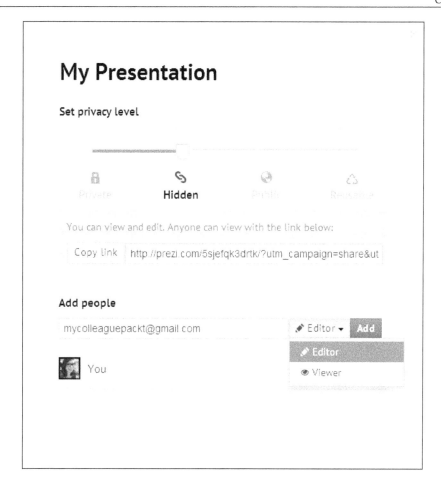

4. Make sure the drop-down option has **Editor** selected.

5. Finally, click on the **Add** button to confirm your selections.

By adding a new editor, an e-mail will be sent to them in order to notify the person you wish to invite to edit a Prezi presentation. If the individual does not have a Prezi account, or if they don't have an account registered to the e-mail address, then you have to send an invitation to the individual and wait for them to sign up. Otherwise, you should see them appear in the list of people under the **Add** option.

When adding someone as an editor, you may have also noticed that you can add them as a viewer. This option is great if you want to limit who can see the presentation to specific individuals. One example of how you might use this is if the presentation had sensitive information and you wanted to restrict access to it. You might also want to control viewers if you wanted others to proofread but not edit the presentation before it is delivered.

The method described in the previous steps is not the only way to access the share settings pop-up window; this can also be accessed from the **Your prezis** home screen. Rather than clicking on the title of the Prezi you wish to add an editor to, simply hover your mouse over the thumbnail preview. This will cause a number of icons to become imposed over the top of this preview; clicking on the icon of a curved arrow next to the **Edit** button will launch the sharing pop-up window.

As the project progresses, or perhaps due to changes in your contacts, you may wish to remove editors. This can be done by opening the sharing pop-up window as we did in the previous steps. You then need to navigate to the list of editors and viewers at the bottom and click on the person you wish to remove. This will bring up a list of options, including one to delete them, as shown in the following screenshot:

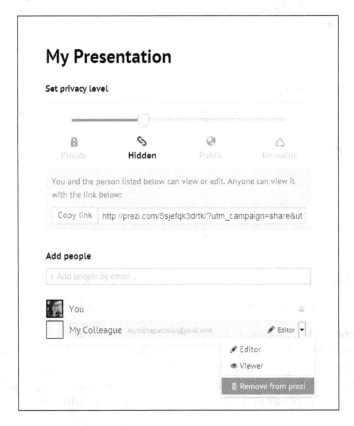

 Clicking on **Remove from prezi** will only remove the editors from this presentation; if you have added them to any other presentation, you will need to remove them from those separately.

Editing as a group

Once you have added co-editors, you will be able to edit your presentation both separately and as a group at the same time. This is one of the unique and highly beneficial features of collaborating via Prezi. This experience will be further enhanced if you use a peer-to-peer networking tool to voice chat or instant message (such as Skype or Google Hangout).

When you are viewing the Prezi canvas at the same time as others, to the right-hand side of the screen will be a thin dark panel. At the top of this panel, it will list how many people are currently editing the presentation (including you) and underneath, it will list those individuals, alongside their profile pictures. You can hover your mouse over any picture to see the name of that individual, if you are unsure. This is demonstrated in the following screenshot:

There is also a plus symbol, which you can click on to invite additional editors to contribute.

When everybody starts editing the presentation, their icons will be super-imposed over the Prezi canvas to show which section they are currently editing. Each user's icon (their profile picture) will move around the canvas as they do. This means you can easily track who is doing what and also ensure you don't step on each other's toes.

It is possible to have 10 individuals editing simultaneously, which makes working as a group on a project quite easy. Remember, if you need to allow for more editors, then you can also remove users and add new ones; so, as people become relevant to the project or complete their tasks, you can reflect this in the user list of the Prezi.

Sharing presentations

Inviting collaborators is not the only way to share your Prezi with your desired audience. You can also change the privacy level on your presentation and share it via a URL. There are four different levels of access, as shown in the following screenshot:

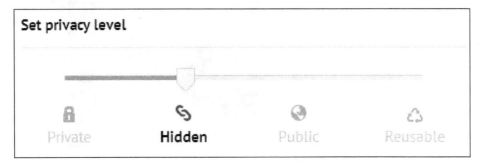

There are different grades of privacy and each grade has a different level of access. **Hidden** is the default option for a new presentation, but the four privacy options allow the following permissions:

- **Private**: Only you can see the presentation. It is useful for drafts or confidential content.

- **Hidden**: Only those you invite or share the link with can see the presentation. This should be used for confidential information that needs to be shared with a colleague, co-editor, or client.

- **Public**: Anyone can see or search for the presentation. This could be used for promotional content.

- **Reusable**: Anyone can see the presentation and take a copy of it to modify for their own use. This is useful if you want to share content more widely, perhaps promotionally, or perhaps in order to gain content in return.

The graduated nature of the privacy options means that they should suit most situations. It is also important to remember that the privacy level is applied on an individual Prezi basis, rather than to all presentations, in the profile settings. You can also create a copy of your own presentation (there is a button to do this, located under the preview window next to the **Share** button) and have a different level of access applied to the copied version. This is shown in the following screenshot:

So, for example, if you had a presentation you wanted to share publicly but couldn't because it contained sensitive or confidential information, then an alternative would be to create a copy of the presentation, edit it to remove the sensitive information, and then make the copied version public. The original version containing the confidential information would independently remain private or hidden except for those specific individuals to whom you have given access.

Present remotely

Once you have finished building your presentation, you can present it as a team as well. The ability to add co-presenters can be a great help if you are working collaboratively. Anyone who has been previously added to the presentation as an editor will be eligible to co-present. This feature can be accessed via the online presentation option. In the following steps, we will look at how to launch this feature, but you will need a co-editor to be online at the same time to utilize it.

If you do not currently have someone you can work with, then please read this section for information but also feel free to return to it when you do have a collaborator.

1. To access the online presentation feature, you will need to click on the title of the presentation you wish to use, from the **Your prezis** home screen:

2. Underneath the preview of your Prezi, there are a number of buttons. Click on the button labeled **Present remotely**, as shown in the following screenshot. By pressing this button, you will expand a menu with a number of options:

3. In the expanded menu, you will notice that one of the options is a URL you can share with those you wish to present online to. To begin presenting online with co-presenters, you must click on the button marked **Start remote presentation**:

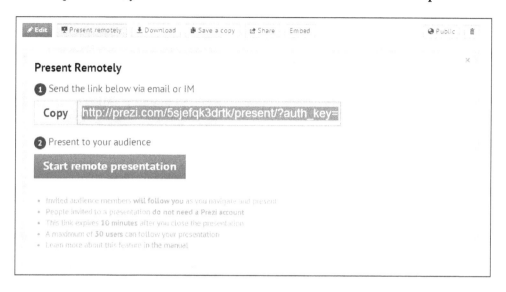

4. This will launch the presentation and you will notice there is a thin side panel to the right of the main canvas. In this panel, you will be able to see who is participating, and also who is eligible to present. Clicking on the profile picture of a co-presenter will give you a number of options such as viewing their profile or zooming in to their location:

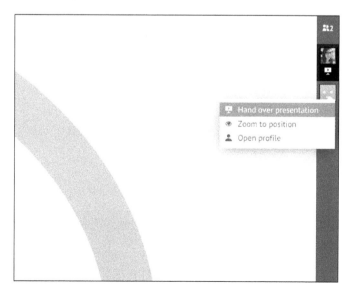

5. If you click on the top of the panel where it noted the number of online participants, you will notice the panel expand outwards and there are some more options. These options include the ability to invite more participants and to stop presenting online:

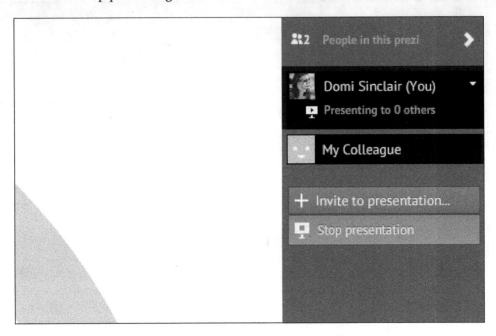

You can present online to a maximum of 30 viewers per session; thus, if you have a large audience, you may need to run multiple sessions. If this is the case, then the ability to co-present becomes even more useful as you can share the tasks of both presenting and answering questions with people you have added as co-editors.

Summary

In this chapter, we have seen how useful working collaboratively can be and how easily Prezi can facilitate it. We looked at how to create a presentation as a team, a function that allows you to delegate different sections or roles to team members, enabling everyone to bring their own expertise to the project. Next, we moved on to explore the other ways Prezi allows you to share a presentation, including making it reusable, which could be useful if you wanted to share something as an open resource. It might also be useful if you were a designer creating stylish and highly designed templates for clients to use and fill with content themselves. Finally, we looked at how to co-present to an online audience, meaning that you can take the collaborative aspects all the way from start to finish in a Prezi project.

This final chapter marks the end of the book but it does not mark the end of your Prezi journey. At the beginning of this book, we talked about how learning and working with any new tool, including Prezi, is a journey, and this book is simply a step along the way. You should now have all the tools you need to work with Prezi, but how you use these skills is up to you. Together we have gone from how to create a new presentation, be that from a template or from scratch, and how to add both basic and complex content to it. We have also explored how to customize the look and edit CSS code for elements of your presentation. Finally, we have just discussed how you can really utilize the online nature of Prezi by using real-time collaborations and easy sharing. This book has taught you what you need to know about Prezi and hopefully inspired some of your own creative ideas.

Good luck!

Index

Thank you for buying
Prezi Essentials

About Packt Publishing

Packt, pronounced 'packed', published its first book "*Mastering phpMyAdmin for Effective MySQL Management*" in April 2004 and subsequently continued to specialize in publishing highly focused books on specific technologies and solutions.

Our books and publications share the experiences of your fellow IT professionals in adapting and customizing today's systems, applications, and frameworks. Our solution based books give you the knowledge and power to customize the software and technologies you're using to get the job done. Packt books are more specific and less general than the IT books you have seen in the past. Our unique business model allows us to bring you more focused information, giving you more of what you need to know, and less of what you don't.

Packt is a modern, yet unique publishing company, which focuses on producing quality, cutting-edge books for communities of developers, administrators, and newbies alike. For more information, please visit our website: www.packtpub.com.

Writing for Packt

We welcome all inquiries from people who are interested in authoring. Book proposals should be sent to author@packtpub.com. If your book idea is still at an early stage and you would like to discuss it first before writing a formal book proposal, contact us; one of our commissioning editors will get in touch with you.

We're not just looking for published authors; if you have strong technical skills but no writing experience, our experienced editors can help you develop a writing career, or simply get some additional reward for your expertise.

Instant Prezi Starter

ISBN: 978-1-84969-702-6   Paperback: 56 pages

A user-friendly, step-by-step introductory guide
to using Prezi, a web-based presentation application
program ideal for engaging your audience

1. Learn something new in an Instant! A short, fast,
   focused guide delivering immediate results.

2. Amaze your audience and keep them engaged
   during your presentations with Prezi.

3. Learn with the help of practical resources
   for awesome examples and inspiration.

Prezi HOTSHOT

ISBN: 978-1-84969-977-8   Paperback: 264 pages

Create amazing Prezi presentations through 10 exciting
Prezi projects

1. Amaze your audience and keep them engaged
   during your presentations with Prezi.

2. Create interactive presentations from scratch
   by adding images, animations, and more.

3. Learn Prezi through ten exciting projects in this
   step-by-step tutorial.

Please check **www.PacktPub.com** for information on our titles